Teaching Shakespeare and Marlowe

Shakespeare Now!
Series edited by Ewan Fernie and Simon Palfrey
Web editors: Theodora Papadopoulou and William McKenzie

First Wave:
At the Bottom of Shakespeare's Ocean Steve Mentz
Godless Shakespeare Eric S. Mallin
Shakespeare's Double Helix Henry S. Turner
Shakespeare Inside Amy Scott-Douglass
Shakespearean Metaphysics Michael Witmore
Shakespeare's Modern Collaborators Lukas Erne
Shakespeare Thinking Philip Davis
To Be Or Not To Be Douglas Bruster

Second Wave:
The King and I Philippa Kelly
The Life in the Sonnets David Fuller
Hamlet's Dreams David Schalkwyk
Nine Lives of William Shakespeare Graham Holderness
Shakespeare and I edited by Theodora Papadopoulou and
   William McKenzie

Visit the *Shakespeare Now!* Blog at http://shakespearenowseries
.blogspot.com/ for further news and updates on the series.

Teaching Shakespeare and Marlowe

Learning vs. the System

LIAM E. SEMLER

B L O O M S B U R Y
LONDON • NEW DELHI • NEW YORK • SYDNEY

Bloomsbury Arden Shakespeare

An imprint of Bloomsbury Publishing Plc

50 Bedford Square
London
WC1B 3DP
UK

1385 Broadway
New York
NY 10018
USA

www.bloomsbury.com

**Bloomsbury is a registered trade mark of
Bloomsbury Publishing PLC**

British Library Cataloguing-in-Publication Data
A catalogue record for this book is available from the British Library.

PB: 978-1-4081-8502-5
ePDF: 978-1-4081-8414-1
ePub: 978-1-4081-8522-3

Library of Congress Cataloging-in-Publication Data
Semler, L. E.
Teaching Shakespeare and Marlowe : learning vs. the system / Liam Semler.
pages cm
Includes bibliographical references and index.
ISBN 978-1-4081-8502-5—ISBN 978-1-4081-8389-2—
ISBN 978-1-4081-8414-1—ISBN 978-1-4081-8522-3
1. Shakespeare, William, 1564-1616—Study and teaching.
2. Marlowe, Christopher, 1564-1593—Study and teaching.
3. Drama—Study and teaching. I. Title.
PR2987.S395 2014
822.3'3—dc23
2013021378

Typeset by RefineCatch Limited, Bungay, Suffolk
Printed and bound in India

To my beloved children,
System Stress, Positive Turbulence and Emergence,
you know who you are —
but not what you may become

CONTENTS

ACKNOWLEDGEMENTS

Thanks to: The 'Shakespeare Reloaded' and 'Better Strangers' teams including Ben Batchen, Linzy Brady, Will Christie, Shauna Colnan, Greg Cunningham, Kate Flaherty, Penny Gay, Claire Hansen, Andrew Hood, Rod Kefford, Lucy Solomon, David Stewart, and all the staff of the English and Drama Departments at Barker College. Thanks also to Margaret Bartley, Matthew Brittain, Ian David, Ewan Fernie, Rebecca Johinke, Jackie Manuel, Simon Palfrey, Brigid Rooney, Alison Scott, Amy Scott-Douglass, Jan Shaw and Peter Wilkin. Special thanks to the Australian Research Council, Barker College and the University of Sydney for co-funding the 'Shakespeare Reloaded' project (2008–10; ARC proj. num. LP0882082); and to Barker College and the University for supporting 'Better Strangers' (2011–13). Warmest thanks (and apologies!) to all the students in the Marlowe module in 2009 and 2011, including Harry Knight, Kira Legaan and Bronwyn O'Reilly.

GENERAL EDITORS' PREFACE TO THE SECOND-WAVE OF THE SERIES

We begin with the passions of the critic as they are forged and explored in Shakespeare. These books speak directly from that fundamental experience of losing and remaking yourself in art. This does not imply, necessarily, a lonely existentialism; the story of a self is always bound up in other stories, shared tales of nations or faiths or of families large and small. But such stories are also always singular, irreducible to the generalities by which they are typically explained. Here, then, is where literary experience stops pretending to provide institutionalized objectivity, and starts to tell its own story.

Shakespeare Now! is a rallying cry, above all for aesthetic immediacy. It favours a model of aesthetic knowledge as *encounter* , where the encounter brings its own, often surprising contextualizing imperatives. Implicit in this is the premise that art is as much a subject as an object, less like aggregated facts and more like a fascinating person or persons. And encountering the plays as such is unavoidably personal.

Much recent scholarship has been devoted to Shakespeare *then* – to producing more information about the presumed moment of their inception. But this moment of inception is in truth happening over and over, again and again, anywhere that Shakespeare is being experienced anew or freshly. For the fact is that he remains, by a country mile, the most important *contemporary* writer – the most performed and read, the most written about, but also the most remembered. But it is not a question merely of Shakespeare in the present, as though his vitality is best measured by his passing relevance to great events. It is about his works' abiding *presence* .

In some ways criticism needs to get younger – to recover the freshness of aesthetic experience, and so in part better to remember why any of us should care. We need a new directness, written responses to the plays which attest to the life we find in them and the life they find in us.

Ewan Fernie and Simon Palfrey

PROLOGUE

This is a book about educational systems – and how they prevent learning. It is about what it means to teach literature, specifically texts by Shakespeare and his contemporary Christopher Marlowe, within large institutional structures such as schools and universities. The relevance of the discussion extends beyond Literary Studies because it is about formal learning systems in general – school and university, curriculum and assessment, disciplines and methodologies – and how they shape our thinking. Most people have been formal students at some point and many of us are either students or teachers now. All teachers and students within educational institutions are agents of systems.

System logics permeate us and influence our perceptions of knowledge, habits of thought and modes of practice. They tell us what is important and what nonsense. They maintain an ethico-intellectual status quo that lays claim to the good. They impel us to assign values to the ideas we encounter and they fuel our automatic eruptions of scorn towards 'manifestly' absurd or wrongheaded notions. I hope this book has more than its fair share of such notions.

What does it mean to teach Shakespeare now? For me, this is not a question of historicism versus formalism or 'active' versus 'desk-bound' approaches. Rather, it is a system question. What does it mean to teach Shakespeare in a world where educational institutions are increasingly driven by formal procedures that coercively standardize, itemize and instrumentalize teaching and learning? What are students and teachers now that schools and universities worldwide have adopted a mode of professional teaching and learning that depends on micro-managerial business models? It is urgent that we stop to ask: what is learning now? If we don't, we risk losing our footing as educators and being swept away by an audit culture that leaves our precious fields of literature (and other fields too) bereft of their natural vitality.

The poetic richness of the Shakespearean text makes it simultaneously the great love of formal learning systems and an indomitable opposite to their reductive systematization. This book begins with some scene-setting that places schools and universities in a matrix of measurement and compliance systems that are state-imposed and market-integrated. It then tightens its focus to explore how Shakespeare is 'schooled' within a modern school curriculum. A specific pedagogical system is examined – the senior-high English curriculum in Australia's most populous state, New South Wales – to illustrate a global phenomenon. The analysis suggests that highly evolved learning systems are weakened by their own side effects and for genuine learning to occur within them a certain posture of unlearning is required. My argument pursues this line, seeking inspiration along the way from Shakespeare's *Sonnets* and *As You Like It*, and trialling solutions through a collaborative project between the University of Sydney and a school.

With unlearning unleashed, who better to push the thesis to its limits than that dogged radical, Christopher Marlowe? Having begun with Shakespeare locked down in the school curriculum and then moved to suggest collaborative modes of release, the argument enters the university classroom to tease its system protocols via consideration of how students and I have been learning – that is to say, unlearning – Marlowe in a tertiary module. As a case study, my experience reveals some of the constraints on learning at university and some of the stresses and possibilities activated by strategically bucking the system.

This is a book about the educator – the school teacher and the academic – caught in a professional bind between system and imagination or, to use a related binary, between standardization and the ineffable, at a time when bureaucratic interference in pedagogical space is peaking. I do not intend to oversimplify, nor do I pretend to solve, the problem. This is not a 'how-to' or 'seven steps to success' book. Rather, the aim is to illuminate various aspects of a global conundrum and to leverage it a little to see what gives.

The texts of Shakespeare and Marlowe are not merely objects of study caught in the abstract web of institutional education; they are replete with parables of learning which can stimulate complex reappraisal of our professional roles. So, to set the scene of the system-vexed school teacher and academic, consider Shakespeare's Hubert and Marlowe's Faustus.

In Shakespeare's play *King John* (4.1) Hubert is sent by John to blind the boy Arthur who is nephew to the king and a claimant to the throne. The scene is a prison, but think of it as a classroom. The absent King John stands for the implacable and distant authority of the institution, an authority that forces processes through system agents onto vulnerable human subjects in order to maintain the status quo. Young Prince Arthur is the malleable student and Hubert, let's call him Mr Hubert, is the teacher. Mr Hubert's role is not easy: he has come to impose a curriculum – made visible as a hot iron poker – that will permanently reshape the boy's perception of the world. Education is a type of eye surgery. Like any operation on the body, it is an act of violence that deforms and forms the patient. Arthur is resistant, he fears loss of agency and dreams to be 'out of prison' and 'as merry as the day is long' (4.1.17–18).[1]

Students know they cannot alter the overarching institutional system enveloping them, but the classroom teacher, by virtue of his or her humanity and proximity, can be reasoned with. Arthur pleads: 'Is there no remedy?' Mr Hubert replies: 'None but to lose your eyes' (89–90). Arthur appeals to their common humanity and shared recognition of what a 'precious sense' sight is (91–5): 'O, spare mine eyes' (101).

Arthur's persistent derailing of the lesson through precocious interjections allows the hot iron to cool: 'Lo, by my

troth, the instrument is cold, / And would not harm me'
(103–4). The resourceful Mr Hubert replies, 'I can heat it,
boy' (105), or more tellingly, 'with my breath I can revive it'
(111). The point is the curriculum is an inert tool in the scene
of education till implemented, actioned, given life by the
teacher. Curricula do not leap unassisted into minds, nor
pokers into eyes. Human breath and will in service of the
instrument are required. And by this stage Mr Hubert lacks
all enthusiasm for his task: he cannot re-heat the iron because,
as Arthur explains, the very fire itself has now gone out 'with
grief' (106).

Worn down by the humanity he shares with his student,
Mr Hubert abandons his system task. The teacher has gone
rogue on behalf of his student and won our admiration in the
process. Space does not permit pursuit of the analogy through
the misprisions that follow and the unfortunate death of
Arthur, but suffice to say these ensuing plot complications
illustrate the rich and untamed complexity of life and all its
accidents beyond, but never entirely free of, the artificial laws
of curriculum.

I've heard students at high school speak just like Arthur: it
is not right, they say, in criticism of the secondary learning
system, to limit forcibly and arbitrarily their experience of the
world of literature. And I've seen teachers at school, as vexed
by their structural subjection as Mr Hubert, inwardly agree
and outwardly subvert their own institutional role as their
system fire goes out. But, as the subsequent adventures of
Hubert and Arthur show, resistance is never simple. Mavericks
in systems cause practical and ethical problems for themselves
and others.

Let's turn to another troubled scene of learning: the famous
opening monologue of Marlowe's Doctor Faustus.[2] We are
witnessing a disciplinary crisis unfold. Dr Faustus is reviewing
some venerable academic disciplines – logic, medicine, law,
theology – and although each one is coherent unto itself he
parodies them because he is disillusioned with the limits of
disciplinarity. In Dr Faustus' jaundiced report, mastery of

logic amounts to little more than polished disputation, medicine falls short of granting resurrection or eternal life, law is 'mercenary,' 'servile' and 'illiberal,' and theology equals fatalism. The disciplines are not internally flawed; it is their finite status as disciplines that disappoints. He belittles them because they don't enable him in the way he desires to be enabled. Dr Faustus has fallen out of empathy with disciplinarity because its proceduralism feels to him like inauthentic learning.

Dr Faustus senses that there is much powerful knowledge beyond traditionally structured systems. He knows that the biggest hurdle is not just believing in the possibility and value of the undisciplined, asystemic, illogical and lawless, but knowing how to think it in order to embrace it. This is the unsolved dilemma of the whole play. It's an academic problem, this one of being troubled by the success of systems, a success partly measured by their invasiveness which makes other knowledges inchoate and unfathomable to the student and teacher alike. Ultimately the problem afflicts every teacher in every formal learning system: it is about how to birth the new.

These are extreme analogies. School teachers do not really terrorize their students and academics do not really damn themselves. However, stark metaphors are required because a great deal is at stake philosophically in education. As teachers within formal systems, we are engaged in practices that shape and limit the way students will perceive the world and we ourselves are shaped and limited by the disciplines enveloping us.[3] We are entangled in formal 'courts' of learning and would benefit greatly from experiences of temporary 'exile.' But exile to where – and how? In the pages below I posit the idea of 'ardenspace' as a valuable destination for system creatures seeking renewal.

What is learning and how free may it be? If we take education seriously, Mr Hubert and Dr Faustus present us with intellectual and practical dilemmas that require urgent consideration. This book attempts that consideration.

PART ONE

Schooling Shakespeare

CHAPTER ONE

Revenge effects

(How systems eat us for breakfast)

2006: It's duck season

I teach in the Department of English at the University of Sydney in Australia. In 2006 I was faced, probably for the first time, with a choice between professional nobility and debasement that reminded me of Shakespeare's poet-lover in the *Sonnets*. I loved the eternal perfection of literature as Shakespeare's persona loves the golden-haired Youth in Sonnet 18.[1] Literary Studies felt like a marriage between me and books that admitted no impediments (Sonnet 116). In university English departments we know our all-too-precious worth, we love the sparkling brightness of our eyes, and will not sell cheap what is most dear. We refuse to acknowledge time's bending sickle (Sonnets 1, 86, 110, 116). We are in perfect empathy with our discipline, but it is out of sync with the world. Winds of change are stirring. We have some lingering credit and are not fully scorned, but we are a discipline disciplined, under review and required to change. Or at least required to explain ourselves.

Again.

And again.

What's our point again? Is it just reading books? What's our contribution – in dollar terms please? And why do the usual rules not apply to us? You know, the ones where we all pay our way. Where disciplines give something back. You know, to be sustainable. We can't always be carried by society, can we? No, of course, we all know that.

I was comically virginal in my devotion to English. Yet my faith had cracks and I found myself drawn to a darker principle. Shakespeare's 'dark lady' (Sonnets 127, 144), an irresistible *femme fatale*, appeared in the form of a dream of corporate engagement. An attraction to infidelity rose inside me. I watched myself, fascinated by the spectacle, falling toward compliance with what I now think of as the university's 'native duck principle.'

I'll explain. At a grant information session with colleagues I heard the following pitch from the university executive to the academics. It went like this. We all agree that Sydneysiders love the Pacific Black Duck which is a local denizen of our parks and waterways. It's a delightful creature, so soft and natty, a feathered brown suitcase of confidence. But it is a threatened species, rather like the humanities academic, and we must all work together to nurture this vulnerable creature. Feeding it is no good because it will become dependent on handouts and forget how to survive in the wild. It is better that governments and universities restrain their natural compassion towards the humanities because that way we who work in the humanities will become strong and develop the necessary skills to thrive in a corporate world. And so, for the time being, the money continues to rush past us on its way to the bustling, productive and demonstrably useful City of STEM (science, technology, engineering and mathematics).

What is *our* point again? Time to rethink.

The universities are increasingly starved of sovereign – that is, public – funding. The 'native duck principle' is being applied unevenly and with uneven impacts across all disciplines. Higher education institutions are prospecting like never before to find and channel corporate – that is, private – funding streams on which to float dehydrated ducks. The Australian government's peak research funding body, the

Australian Research Council (ARC), has a 'Linkage Projects' grant scheme specifically designed to support such ventures. It describes itself as aiming

> to support research and development projects which are collaborative between higher education researchers and other parts of the national innovation system, which are undertaken to acquire new knowledge, and which involve risk or innovation. Proposals for funding under the *Linkage Projects* scheme must include at least one Australian Partner Organisation.[2]

In a Linkage Projects grant application, the cash contribution promised to the project by the non-tertiary Partner Organization (PO) should be equal to at least 20 per cent of the total amount of cash requested from the ARC. The PO must also deliver 'in-kind' (non-cash) contributions at least equal to the remaining 80 per cent. This means that if the project seeks $500,000 from the ARC, it will need (in addition) to seek at least $100,000 from the PO in real money over the life of the project, as well as in-kind contributions (such as a proportion of PO staff salary and infrastructure costs) equaling at least $400,000. The total cash and in-kind budget would then be a least $1,000,000 in this example. Various permutations might apply such as options for multiple POs or multiple universities on a single project, and waivers and exemptions in special circumstances. It's an ingenious framework.

The scheme works well for SciTech faculties – offering another formal structure, among many already in place, within which their normal, collaborative research operations can thrive. It's more difficult for humanities and English Literature to attract industry partners. Art galleries and book publishers, theatres and cultural festivals, state schools and community associations – basically all our friends are dead broke. And plenty of us don't want any 'stakeholder' friends putting their noses in our research anyway.

If you combine our potential partners' pennilessness with our reluctance to strike deals, you have a winning combination in a race to the bottom of the future. In any year's list of Linkage Projects funding outcomes, the successful projects are primarily based in the sciences. The humanities' successes are more isolated and idiosyncratic. Universities and governments would like to see more effective commercialization of the humanities with more private money on the table, through Linkage or other schemes, to fund Arts research. This challenge began to possess me.

2011–13: The comfort and despair of systems

The sorts of research projects that I and my colleagues prefer are 'sole-trader' operations where lone investigators conduct detailed archival, analytical or theoretical work of importance in the field of Literary Studies, leading to production of peer-reviewed articles and eventually monograph publications. To fund these manifestations of academic research identity we usually apply for ARC 'Discovery Project' grants. In many Australian universities the staff are all but compelled to submit such applications. This would be fine perhaps, except that the application process takes about as much time as it would take to write a chapter in one's gradually emerging monograph and the success rate annually within 'Humanities and Creative Arts' is about 20 per cent of applicants. This means that at the end of each year when Discovery Project outcomes are announced about 80 per cent of applicants – and much higher if we just consider the 'Literary Studies' subcategory – are feeling like kicked dogs. Then term recommences, classroom teaching obliterates research headspace, the monograph is no nearer completion, and the researcher has a refreshed quantum of professional despair.

My colleagues and I are being munched by the global mania for league table positioning, which is to say, eaten by formula. Formulae are systems' teeth. Educational institutions have more teeth now than they've ever had, and more are coming through, more than they know what to chew with. The 'revenge effect' of these systems is the fact that they can only chew their own agents. Revenge effects are the obstacles, often on a catastrophic scale, to a system's principles and processes that have been called into being by that very system.[3] Look at academia now: we live in the age of wisdom teeth and edible academics. School teachers were eaten long ago. They are living an extended burp that provokes endless disapproving looks.

Australia has entered a new era of extraordinary, systemic alignment in tertiary and secondary education. An immaculately crafted pedagogical shark is gliding into view with row upon row of perfectly set and incrementally gauged teeth. 'It's just a pure teaching machine!' cry terrified beach-goers. They swim for their lives, but there's no escape. At university, projected 'learning outcomes' for individual *modules* of study match with *course* 'pathways' and rationales for *majors* which align with *degree* 'learning objectives' and *university* 'graduate attributes.' Learning systems are seeking institutional, national and international parities: semesterial, modularized, benchmarked, standardized, commoditized, mono-jargonized, exchangeable. As any follower of the Bologna Process and other large standardizing trends will know, these features are becoming increasingly naturalized in tertiary institutions. In some respects this has improved teaching and learning, but it is perhaps truer to say the avalanche of invasive policies and procedures is causing specific types of teaching and learning and specific types of educators and students. Lines of causality are becoming ever more finely articulated, ever more predictable, abstracted and irresistible. This means more and more effects are becoming uncausable and gradually unthinkable. Where lies the uncaused? It lies all about us, beyond the dot points of the audit culture, in a vast, profound and growing 'dark matter' of teaching and learning possibilities. Out of sight, out of mind.

In Australia, the 'My School' and 'My University' websites offer potential students, parents and other stakeholders a battery of government provided statistics and comparative chart-making possibilities via which to draw variously dodgy conclusions about the merits and demerits of various institutions and their staff. It is DIY league tabling for student and parent clients who want to make 'informed' decisions with 'authoritative' data about their education provider.[4]

On the My School site one can view any school's achievement levels in various learning areas year on year via graphed results from the National Assessment Program: Literacy and Numeracy (NAPLAN). According to the NAPLAN website, NAPLAN 'is an annual assessment for students in Years 3, 5, 7 and 9' that 'tests the sorts of skills that are essential for every child to progress through school and life, such as reading, writing, spelling and numeracy.' Although the National Assessment Program (NAP) website says in anxious, bold lettering that 'NAPLAN tests are not tests students can prepare for,' this statement is disingenuous. It manifests a philosophical denial of the artificial nature of the testing process, and a concrete denial of wide-scale 'teaching to the test' in classrooms and the existence of an array of commercially available NAPLAN primers that worried parents buy to drill their worried children on. One publisher has reportedly sold-out four times in four months its 60,000 print run of NAPLAN primers for Years 3 and 5 (boasting bright colours and sticker rewards) (Macdonald). NAPLAN outcomes matter because government can thereby bring more precise pressure to bear on individual schools over specific results, and teachers are in the firing line too as moves are afoot to implement 'performance' or 'merit' pay.

A recent study explains how neoliberal educational narratives are promulgated in the print media reporting of the My School website: distrust of teachers is manifested via deployment of supposedly transparent and useful data to keep them accountable; the public provision of the data serves a controlled narrative of informed, free choice for consumers (such as parents); and the datasets embed unhelpful competitiveness and skew pedagogical activity that becomes driven by abstract charts and figures rather than by educational principles.[5]

The USA, UK and Australia are among many nations experiencing this sovereign push to make teacher pay scales depend on official measurement of teachers' supposed success or failure in causing definable levels of learning in students as demonstrated via formal evaluation methods. Massive strike action has greeted, but not halted, this growing trend. It makes me, as an academic, think of the increasing institutional weight being given to officially managed student evaluations of tertiary teachers and teaching. Even when we set aside formal systems' tendency towards hubristic assertions about what is 'essential' for 'progress' in 'life,' there remains the unsettling presumption that there is a transparent and natural relationship between each of these terms: education and measurement and evaluation and remuneration and professionalization. These are system fictions typical of formal education in our time. The absurdity of the situation lies in the system's childlike absolutism as it replaces the core of a profession with a manageable spectre and is satisfied with procedural compliance rather than principled professional engagement and commitment. It is absolutely to the point that this culture, as Greg Thompson and Ian Cook brilliantly show, is bringing into being a new type of teacher and principal – one who willingly 'cheats' the audit system and manipulates the data because the system is seen to be amoral or even immoral and its requirements to be entirely distinct from the ethics of good teaching in the classroom.[6]

In 2013 Australia's first fully national curriculum from K-12 (the 'Australian Curriculum') is nearing its final stages of construction under the auspices of the Australian Curriculum, Assessment and Reporting Authority (ACARA), before implementation across all states and territories which to date have taught students their own way. While the state of New South Wales has created its new K-10 English syllabus in accord with the Australian Curriculum (for implementation from 2014), it has roundly critiqued the draft national framework for senior-high English and currently plans to continue using its state-based system for the final two years of school.

From 2012 the Tertiary Education Quality Standards Agency (TEQSA) commenced its brief to 'regulate and assure' quality teaching and learning in higher education by measuring all Australian tertiary institutions against a new Higher Education Standards Framework. TEQSA will use this method to perform 'compliance assessments' and 'quality assessments' of universities against 'Threshold Standards' to confirm or query institutions' registration as higher education providers. Immediately relevant to this is the Australian Qualifications Framework (AQF) which describes in detail and by standardized 'AQF Levels' the knowledge, skills and volume of learning required for all tertiary qualifications. While most Australian Universities are falling into line with TEQSA and the AQF, the University of New South Wales has voiced powerful and reasoned opposition to the new regulations and it remains to be seen how its bold complaint about the flaws of coercive, standardizing systems will play out. Another interesting reaction is the Australian Historical Association's attempt to organize its professional community to engage proactively in the standards process from the point of view of the discipline of History.[7]

A further development is the implementation of the first round of 'Mission-Based Compacts' (2011–13) whereby each Australian university has produced a formally binding declaration of its specific 'mission' and strategic 'goals.' Each university's Compact marries its unique 'Strategic Plan' and self-identified 'Research Strengths' to government priorities for higher education nationally. There is substantial 'Reward Funding' for performance achievements in specific areas such as the boosting of low socio-economic student enrolments. Most Australian universities are now scrambling to maximize their financial and public relations returns via fast-tracked compliance with their Compacts, the AQF and TEQSA's Standards Framework.

The catch-cry of all these teeth-baring acronyms is quality, transparency, sustainability and professionalism. Lord help you if you swim outside the flags. The ideal is that you should be able to give any graduate of any university or school a good shake whereupon six dot points encapsulating their knowledge identity will tumble out and stand to attention in a way that is globally legible and transferrable. The dot points will be like a crystalline time tunnel, directly connecting the marking criteria of every essay the student has written since the start of their studies to the student's vocational destiny in some worthwhile sector of society.

Who'd have thought that neoliberal education's most devastating ammunition was the dot point? It killed the lecture when fired out of PowerPoint Presentations, it immobilized student learning via lists of 'projected learning outcomes,' and now it is redefining what teachers are by arbitrary lists of what they supposedly (should and must) do. Not only is it disaggregating the teacher (and student and learning) into a list of 'specific, auditable competencies and performances,'[8] but more worrying is the subjective internalization of the dot point rationale as Raewyn Connell observes: 'Under a neoliberal regime, educational institutions must *make themselves auditable*.'[9] Death by dot point is a type of poisoning – of teaching, learning, student, teacher and profession – that produces some spectacularly ghastly public moments.

This situation exemplifies Tyson E. Lewis's argument via Giorgio Agamben that neoliberal education eradicates the freedom of its learners by actualizing their potential as productive citizens within the modern learning society.[10] This actualization amounts to the exhaustion of potential. It is achieved through relentless quantification, standardization and control of learning experiences and outputs. It is a biometrically obsessed institutional process that has the net effect of destroying human potentiality in individuals who become instead efficient, economically viable and self-regulating citizens of neoliberalism. In the terms of my opening analogies from Shakespeare and Marlowe, both Arthur and Faustus resist such crippling actualization – for one, it would have meant loss of ability to see, for the other, incarceration within ideologically inflected discipline boundaries. Instead, both nurture their potential to not be as the system requires in order to retain for themselves the potential to be (or not be) whatever and however they desire. In Agamben's terms, the rejection of coercive actualization returns potential to itself and may be designated the subject's liberating (im)potential. In their attempts to possess (im)potential, Arthur and Faustus respond to cultural coercion with words that value and marry freedom and play – as indeed Agamben does when he posits a pure notion of 'study' as 'serious play' that is decoupled from the efficiencies of instrumental learning and delivers a 'stupefying' excess of possibility, openness and inspiration.

Over-systematization deskills its agents, outsources their thinking and artificializes their activities. The system cores itself unwittingly. Its purposes and ends supplant the purposes and ends of the activity it supposedly guarantees. It cleans by bleaching and facilitates by infantilizing. It steals and imprisons terminology such as 'quality,' 'professional,' 'efficiency,' 'learning,' 'teaching,' 'standards' and 'achievement.' It bestows comfort by creating system animals. In their baskets. In rows. In learned obedience. These revenge effects are galling in the realm of higher education which legitimately yearns for a degree of separation from imposed modes of thought, predestined futures, corporatization and bureaucratization. A significant humanities deficit lies beneath system opulence.[11]

The quality assurance and compliance situation is complicated by the fact that humanities academics are being extruded into the world of commerce to see what crazy deals they can stitch up as governments no longer stop to pick up the Arts. Forget duck season, it's like unleashing swarms of mentally incompetent, over-institutionalized fools on the world of business. Me, for example.

Cry havoc and let slip the dons galore. Someone is bound to get hurt, or worse, hooked. Capitalism is spreading its influence down through governments and universities to cause the emergence of the junkie-academic forever chasing dubious sugar daddies so as to maintain artificially the rush required to operate at the unsustainable level demanded by his or her tertiary employer.

We in the humanities are troubled by all this. It is not how we imagined our discipline or ourselves. Our marriage is in trouble. What exactly is ineffable about our discipline? Where lie the limits of acceptability and truth in our discipline? Is there a disciplinary event horizon, a moral and conceptual point of no return for the humanities beyond which 'Desire is death' and 'black' is falsely avowed 'bright' (Sonnet 147)? Is the boundary crossed when an individual academic is financially supported by a non-tertiary stakeholder? Does he or she become at that point an intolerably 'perjured eye' (Sonnet 152)? A non-academic. An entrepreneur. Rust in the idea of the university.

2011–13: Learning and gaming on the scaffold

My literature students at Sydney University come primarily from schools in the same state, New South Wales (NSW). They do not come alone: they come rich with system. Most have been schooled formally for twelve years and the final two years amount to a capstone in which they are polished into glistening system pats and flung at the walls of higher education. Some make it over. Some splat like mud. Of the ones who make it over, not all land well.

Here's how it works. Every year in NSW a suite of statewide written examinations covering over one hundred Year 12 courses and known as the Higher School Certificate (HSC) is externally prepared by committees of subject-area experts under the control of the NSW Board of Studies. In 2012 there were 73,397 students enrolled in the HSC statewide. Most students sat five or six exam papers across the various HSC courses relevant to their studies and 68,611 sat exams in the one mandatory high school subject, English.[12]

Although 50 per cent of a student's marks come from locally managed assessment tasks during the final year, from a NSW Year 12 student's perspective it is the final exam event that is seen as the most important rendezvous in one's school career. The school year (like the academic year) is a calendar year and the HSC's written examinations occur in October and November, contribute decisively to one's university entrance ranking, and are often experienced as an intensely stressful and high-stakes operation that sometimes has deleterious effects on personal life. In 2008 the Board of Studies released a discussion paper acknowledging concerns about over-assessment and exam pressure contributing to student stress levels. No other Australian state or territory's final year examination system sows such anxiety among students and their families. It is a coming-of-age ritual in NSW that is accompanied by media hype and innumerable published guides to achieving success or maintaining sanity.[13] It is followed by 'Schoolies Week,' a carnival of misrule where thousands of delirious eighteen-year-olds head for Surfers Paradise in Queensland to drink themselves stupid and write-off their parents' cars.

Supposing they survive their exams and the after-party, Australian students who enter the nation's universities do so with a state-inflected, and hence nationally discontinuous, range of skills and knowledge in any discipline. First year at university is, among other things, a year of debriefing and realignment of the student mind so that by about second year all tertiary students nationally in any one subject area are more or less 'on the same page' in terms of approach, methodology and practice, even if their school experience and equipping were diverse. The forthcoming Australian Curriculum hopes to level the field at school by defining nationally uniform, Stage-designated, minimal 'learning entitlements' within subject areas from K-12.

Senior English in NSW schools is such a 'scaffolded' or micro-structured educational system that teachers who move into NSW from other Australian states are sometimes aghast at the complexity of the mechanism, the abundance of tailor-made curriculum resources and the lack of freedom for students and teachers who are all enmeshed in a labyrinth of protocols and requirements to which they must react in limited time constraints. Such perceptions are, of course, relative, but the dense weave of this system's internal regulations, including its high-stakes final examination, makes it susceptible to 'backwash.'

Backwash refers to the student learning experience being unduly inflected by students' and teachers' perceptions of syllabus-based assessment requirements.[14] John Biggs and Catherine Tang observe that: 'Negative backwash always occurs in an exam-dominated system. Strategy becomes more important than substance. Teachers actually teach exam-taking strategies. . . . This sort of backwash leads inevitably to surface learning.'[15] If reports about the way teachers, students and parents strategically prepare for NAPLAN testing in Years 3, 5, 7 and 9 are true, then Australian formal learning systems are awash with backwash even before a NSW student arrives at the HSC.

Kim Jagger, principal of the selective school, Sydney Boys' High, believes the HSC examination system, particularly in respect to English, because of its highly prescribed, objectives-based learning methodology and its level of predictability from year to year, 'produces a sort of decadence' as teachers and students 'learn faster how to play the game.'[16] Jagger wants more 'surprises' in the final exam, otherwise schools, students, parents, private tutors and publishers of study guides will collectively work the system at its weakest points. Students will 'end up with the best assessment product that money can buy' because those who can financially afford strategic tutors will employ them and those who can morally afford purchase of pre-written, generic essays for memorization, regurgitation and modification in the exam, will acquire them.[17] This strategic, success-oriented approach is sometimes designated 'achieving learning' where the student seeks to achieve the best possible grades in the educational system by doing whatever it takes to score well: at times this may require deployment of 'surface' or 'deep' approaches.

'Surface learning' is characterized by use of lower order cognition and a student's desire to meet the course requirements as effortlessly as possible. It relies on memorization and reproduction of piecemeal content, listing of undigested topics and thoughtless regurgitation of quotations perceived by students to be valued by markers. Teaching and learning schemes that encourage surface learning are often seen as dryly mechanical by students who can, in turn, respond with calculated surface-learning strategies that have the capacity to confirm their cynicism by delivering them good marks. Such students are disengaged from authentic learning during the process and retrospectively scornful of their 'learning' experience.

'Deep learning,' by contrast, is characterized by higher order cognition, authentic engagement and active reflection on and manipulation of knowledge resulting in the student's formulation of new theories and hypotheses. Students who engage in deep learning want to be able to demonstrate it in the examination room and are particularly frustrated if the assessment regime sabotages this.[18]

Gaming of the system is particularly prevalent among students at private and selective schools whose families are paying big money for their children's 'education' and many of whose students are seeking marks in the 95–100 percentile range in order to enter their desired, top-flight university degrees. Timothy Large, who topped the state in 'Extension 2 Mathematics' in 2011, observed that in NSW many students have stopped thinking of 'education as education and have started thinking of education – in particular the HSC and in particular in subjects like mathematics – as education for getting marks.'[19] Harry Stratton who topped Classical Greek and Latin feels that 'to some extent gaming the system is inevitable, particularly when you place high stakes on one exam like HSC English.' Tom Alegounarias, president of the NSW Board of Studies, is aware that all major examination systems must be alert to gaming strategies, but says that the boundary between appropriate preparation and gaming is not as clear as the HSC's critics might think. He feels that the 'really outstanding students will mix memorizing with originality' and that there's little 'the Board can do to stop gaming when people are really dedicated to gaming the system.' Purists may not like Alegounarias' remarks, but his words are astute.

Where lies the definitional boundary between learning and gaming? If the system declares itself to be a fair and worthwhile educational system then effective facilitation of learning is its aim and it will want to minimize the detrimental impact of its own system noise on this aim. You can fine-tune system processes to militate against gaming strategies in order to facilitate more equitable and pedagogically sound outcomes to students. The problem is that the system grows in subroutines as it strives to turn down its static – and the more subroutines, the more static.

Revenge effects abound as system noise spills in all directions. For example, overly structured educational institutions are ultimately not ones that invite teachers to discover what they can become. They declare the ways their agents are to be. When teachers resist, fail or subvert, the system evolves protocols to call them back into line, which in turn causes new displacement activity leading to new containments and so on. Carol Atherton notes how 'the managerial culture in education,' the 'target-driven' approaches to teaching and the 'instrumentalization' of the profession have led to an 'intellectual deskilling' of teachers, an 'intensification' of their workloads and their relative disenfranchisement from cross-institutional, direction-setting discussions of education.[20]

The Board of Studies does not seek to promote surface learning and the current HSC regime, inaugurated in the revolutionary 1999 *English Stage 6 Syllabus*, is considered by many to be a vast improvement on the previous system. Those who work at or for the Board are dedicated educational professionals including teachers, former teachers and academics (myself included). All those I've met are genuinely committed to the intelligent enrichment of student learning and the support of teachers within this large and complex system. I have no quarrel with them in the account that follows because I too am a system-embedded educational professional and my focus below is rather on the philosophical implications of systemic education.

A look at the Board of Studies website reveals just how resourced and self-aware the system is. It endorses the teaching and learning of analytical *and* creative responses to literature and values, both in the classroom and in the assessment regime. Its syllabus documents and examinations are intelligently framed. Its marking processes are validly and sensitively conducted. Its attempts to hear and respond to student, teacher and parent perplexity are genuine and diverse. I mean none of this ironically. You could say its heart is in the right place – but it is a system heart. It has its protocols and sub-protocols to surveil, query, appeal and renew its protocols. It can be authoritative, sincere, empathetic, transparent, complicated, unrelenting and decisive. It is the alpha male of learning systems.

This very fact, its infinite systemness, is its Achilles' heel. The question is fundamental and general: how do educational structures relate to, allow and define learning? At what point does an educational system become over-evolved, too self-conscious and too complicated for its own good? Possibly at the point at which it feels that things cannot be done better another way, or when it can only imagine fine-tuning rather than system overhaul, or when its contradictions or weaknesses become invisible to it. Over-bred pedagogical structures become compulsive hunters of their own anomalies which they subject to neutralization via system-integration for the sake of consistency and system muscle-tone. They are gluttons of reality.

They devote ever more energy to preserving themselves as operative structures and lose sight of, and ability to enact, far simpler truths of teaching and learning. Within such structures teachers and students may become less valued as autonomous agents and more valued as manageable functionaries. Human capacity is elided and reduced and the system's primary directive becomes its own self-preservation. We can call this self-maintenance impulse 'reason of system.' Once teaching and learning are caught in structures governed by reason of system, what do they become and how might they get out? We can address this by examining Shakespeare's position in the HSC.

2006–13: Shakespeare disciplined

How are you doing Shakespeare? In NSW we like him well done. Which is to say done in; or perhaps underdone.

English is a compulsory subject for secondary students in NSW and Shakespeare is currently mandated for study in Stage 5 (school Years 9–10, at about 14–16 years of age) of the English syllabus in the following terms: 'the selection of texts must give students experience of Shakespearean drama.'[21] The earliest that NSW students may leave school is at the age of 17 and so this Shakespeare mandate means no student in NSW can avoid 'experience of Shakespearean drama,' just as they cannot avoid 'the study of Australian literature' and 'the study of Aboriginal experiences and multicultural experiences.'[22] The phraseology leaves it up to individual schools to shape this Shakespeare 'experience': it might mean analyzing or performing extracts from plays or seeing modern appropriations. Often students encounter their first full Shakespeare text in Year 9 or 10, but many schools introduce Shakespeare in some form in the first year of high school (Year 7; 12–13 year olds).

The Board of Studies has ensured that a range of Shakespeare possibilities exists for those who stay on into the two senior years, but any student's options are limited by his or her school's choice of what courses and electives it will teach and by various syllabus requirements internal to courses.[23] The Stage 6 English syllabus governs study in the two senior years (Years 11–12, being 17–18 year olds) and is the so-called 'HSC syllabus' (with Year 11 being the 'preliminary year'). It caters for varying levels of ability, with the lowest level, 'HSC English (Standard),' allowing the possibility (not necessity) of the study of *As You Like It* in terms of 'the concept of belonging' (this is part of the 'Common Content of Standard and Advanced Courses'). Students of 'Standard' also have the chance of studying *The Merchant of Venice* within the Module entitled 'Close Study of a Text.'

In the HSC syllabus, the level above 'Standard' is 'Advanced' and it mandates the study of some example of 'Shakespearean drama' (as one of five compulsory text types) and offers the following alternatives: *Richard III*, paired with Al Pacino's film *Looking for Richard* (1996), under the rubric 'Exploring Connections' (Module A, Elective 1); *Hamlet*, under the rubric 'Critical Study of Texts' which emphasizes the students' development of their own 'informed personal understanding' of the text (Module B); and *Julius Caesar*, under the rubric 'Conflicting Perspectives' (Module C, Elective 1). 'Advanced' students also have the choice of *As You Like It* and the notion of 'belonging' which, if selected, would fulfil their Shakespeare requirement and leave them free to avoid any other Shakespeare options. Finally, for those doing the more academically sophisticated 'English Extension 1' course (who must do 'Advanced' as a co-requisite), there is the possibility of exploring *Twelfth Night* in terms of 'Language and Gender' (Module C, Elective 2).

In sum then, in senior-level English in NSW, 'Standard' students (numbering 32,255 in 2012) can avoid Shakespeare altogether, while 'Advanced' students (27,366), being about 40 per cent of all enrolled HSC English students, will be taught and assessed on some Shakespearean drama. Those 'Advanced' students who decide to do 'Extension 1' (5359) as well, and thus comprise the state's brightest cohort of literature students, have the option of doing *Twelfth Night* at that highest level, but the numbers in this elective are always very small because 'Extension 1' students are far more likely to study more 'modern' electives such as 'Crime Writing' or 'After the Bomb' (a Cold War literature module). There is also an 'Extension 2' course (numbering 2,164 students), which is open to 'Extension 1' students who want to do the maximum amount of English possible for the HSC, and these students may write an extended piece of critical analysis or produce a creative work. Among these, a tiny minority might focus on a Shakespearean theme or text.

This means that as a general rule the state's most able English students, those doing 'Extension 1,' tend not to study or be examined on Shakespeare at that level. However, since they must also do 'Advanced,' they will study Shakespeare at that lower level along with all students doing 'Advanced.' The only way to avoid meeting Shakespeare in the senior years (Stage 6) is to do 'Standard' and rely on the probability that your school is not going to force such a cohort to do the Shakespearean options. It is heartening that many schools do indeed take up the Shakespeare options at 'Standard' level.

It is a virtue of the NSW curriculum that it allows the possibility of studying Shakespeare at every ability level of post-compulsory (Years 11–12) English from 'Standard' up to 'Extension 1' and 'Extension 2.' Furthermore, the mandatory Shakespeare requirement at 'Advanced' level in tandem with the mandatory nature of English succeeds in compelling, ultimately, about 40 per cent of *all* NSW senior-high students, including many who prefer science or mathematics, to study and be examined on Shakespeare. For a country that lionizes sport and is deeply suspicious of Shakespeare's privileged position and anybody's flowery words, this is good going. But it is not good going if this compulsory experience of Shakespeare is a negative one due to system flaws.

An important reservation about the Stage 6 Shakespeare offerings is that in most cases teachers must teach and students must learn the plays in relation to pre-defined thematic frameworks. The frameworks and topics are meant to be generative and engaging fields of exploration for students, but the limitations can soon become oppressive. This is not to say students will not get to know the text of a play *per se*, or learn something of its broad sweep of meanings, but it is to say that students and teachers must give significant, even to some degree primary, attention to prescribed frameworks because classroom time is short and the HSC examination will explicitly assess student learning in relation to them. For example, in 2008 *The Tempest* was explored in terms of 'imaginative journeys' ('Common Content of Standard and Advanced'), and *Hamlet* was explored specifically in relation to Tom Stoppard's *Rosencrantz and Guildenstern are Dead* ('Advanced,' Module A, Elective 1).[24] This meant, among other things, that important aspects of *The Tempest* that did not fit the 'imaginative journey' concept could be ignored and important aspects of *Hamlet*'s historicity were confused by importation of twentieth-century existential terminology.

When a colleague of mine used the word 'journey' unwittingly in a first-year lecture on *The Tempest*, 300 students groaned involuntarily. The lecturer wasn't to know that the notion of 'journey' had tyrannized over many of his students for the duration of Year 12, never allowing them to approach *The Tempest* outside this worked-to-death frame. The word was ruined for them and its invisible toxicity hindered their learning in first-year.

In each module or elective the HSC examination question forces a student to address the text within its prescribed framework and hence student learning of Shakespeare is impacted by a combination of conceptual constraint, class time pressure and backwash. The need to spend teaching time on conceptual frameworks and approaches, which is simultaneously to spend time on examination preparedness and strategy, necessarily limits the time available to explore the text and language of Shakespeare's plays more diversely. Students will undoubtedly learn something, but it may be more a case of learning how to prove the framework true with a series of found examples from the play, than learning how the play itself may lead interpretation in multiple and unexpected directions. In this context, surface learning and cynicism can infect even the more engaged students, not to mention teachers.

Examination room behaviour – be it calm and well-drilled or desperate and confused – is always a type of system responsiveness seeking forms of security. Uncertainty is precisely what senior-high students do not want and they figure quite rightly that they cannot afford the risk of too much solo thought or novelty because the stakes are too high. They do not want to perplex the system; they know they need to make sure the system 'gets' them and their response. They feel far more secure down-valuing their own views, doing what they think everyone else is doing (with a little personal tweaking where possible to stand out), and absorbing page after page of remarks from their teacher whom they view as a fount of all wisdom, or at least as a reliable key to success in examinations. It is far better to give the system what you think it wants than to trip it up so it shoots you dead.

This very weakness – students within exam-dominated pedagogical systems being fearful of taking interpretive risks and thus becoming habituated to, indeed adept at, surface-learning procedures to achieve clearly defined goals – emerges with a vengeance in the first year of university study. Many students arrive ill-practiced at close reading and construction of convincing argument based upon it, and tend to engage in generalizing and superficial displays of assertive declaration. Their work frequently reveals that they lack faith in the poetical words of a text to deliver up sparkling arrays of meaning and connotation and so feel that words and phrases are not worth dwelling on for too long or too deeply. This is a fundamental weakness in preparedness for university English study and academics are often stunned by new students' blindness to the possibilities possessed by words in literary texts. At university, first-year literature students desperately seek to know the answers from lecturers so that they can relay them confidently back to lecturers in assessable work. They are often mystified by how wrong this approach is – not to mention blind to how pointless it is. These students are in the security business, not the learning business, and they don't know it because the two are thoroughly confused. This is the ultimate revenge effect.

CHAPTER TWO

Positive turbulence
(How we fight back)

2008: Not dissing, blessing

Large formal learning systems will always be structured political affairs. Universities and state or nationwide school
systems, with student throughputs in the tens of thousands
and countless teaching staff, will always promote rituals of
teaching and learning. Not all rituals are bad and the sheer
numbers themselves call formality and abstraction into being.
But the liturgy of our age is that every pedagogical move and
response is dogmatically pre-defined, retailed and evaluated
with such faux exactitude that no allowance is made for the
messy ecstasy and mystery of teaching and learning.[1] Hey
dude, where's my rapture? Rapture, are you kidding? This is
learning, not a fun park.

These systems are ideological constructs seeking to perpetuate, reform or establish habits of thought with attendant
knowledge hoards and skill-sets. They are, at some fundamental, societal level, what we want to do to our children.
Everyone has views on how this is best done. Academics are
notorious for criticizing school teachers for failing to prepare
students adequately for tertiary study, just as high school
teachers have been known to criticize primary school teachers

for an analogous failing, and all school teachers have a word or two to say about parents. Blaming someone else is terrifically good for the soul. You can't pass the blame upwards very easily because students move forwards through time as they move upwards through systems. So we spew students upward and defecate complaints downward. Learning for the student can become an uphill struggle through a hail of crap. No fun park.

Is it possible to pour illicit turbulence into learning systems? To upset their fine economies with creative whorls? What are the strategies of blessing given from human to human in spite of system's logics? We need rushes of oxygen and love that uplift and encourage the student. Moments of giving that exceed routines of demand. Petrol poured on talent and beauty on desire. Is it possible to crack the shell of system from within?

Every flaw in the NSW senior-high curriculum and its HSC examination is explicable in terms of politics, economics and/or ideology: but not always in predictable ways. For example, academics like to criticize the 'set text' list for a particular HSC English elective for its odd inclusions and omissions, but do not realize that the Board of Studies cannot simply tell cash-strapped state schools to buy a raft of new texts. The schools just don't have the money. This is the 'bookroom' problem and it in part explains the tragic reappearance of the same texts decade after decade even in newly invented electives. Even if the introduction of an entirely new text is approved for a new elective, its selection is a fraught and laborious process where numerous stakeholders and interest groups have their say on the suggested text's content and appropriateness. This never proceeds smoothly and, like so many of these processes, will result in compromises.

Academics can be naïve on how complicated and compromised any action is in relation to altering the official state education system for school-aged children. This naivety is due to many factors, not least among which are the academics' greater autonomy in the creation of their modules of study and 'set text' lists at university, and the academics' lack of time and headspace to enter into understanding another large educational system when the responsibilities of their own envelop them. Once perceived flaws are understood, their significance (inherently and relative to other features of the system) and capability of being rectified are seen to vary enormously. If academics can get some insight into these matters, they can then make judgments about what needs to be changed, what might be able to be changed, and how changes might be effected. While many educators like to criticize the Board for all manner of evils, those teachers and academics actually involved in duties related to the Board's operations have a far more nuanced and knowledgeable view of the situation in the quagmire.

As someone who co-writes the HSC English 'Extension 1' examination paper, I am aware of the pros and cons of being a part of this massive educational machine. No-one likes exams at the best of times: students, teachers, academics and educational theorists all have something negative to say about them and when one group is appeased another is infuriated.

Given the high-stakes nature of the HSC examination, it must be equitable and valid, it must work against pre-prepared and plagiarized responses, it must have real and apparent parity across electives and from year to year, it must be non-exclusionary and non-offensive, it must enable all students to show what they've learned, it must allow the brightest students to shine, it must be from the centre of the syllabus yet not predictable, it must be free of errors, typos and obscurities, it must fulfil a bunch of musts that are partly artificial and partly not fulfillable, it must . . ., it must . . ., it must. . . .

The exam-writing committee is the servant of 'must' and the slave of system. Its product, the exam paper, is an outcome of necessity, a mere angle caused by converging lines. It is a bare instrument, a product that has no soul, without autochthony or aspiration. It is born, carries greatness briefly, then dies without ever growing up or going outside. It concentrates the system and its subjects in one heightened moment. A moment the system reveres and depends on. It therefore concentrates criticism of the system. To the system's enemies, the exam is its epitome. It turns instruction into malice, suspicion into evidence, regime into crime. The exam is both nothing and everything, bestowing triumph or oblivion on the system's subjects.

It is forgotten that the exam may be beautiful. Like any other piece of this multi-system system, it has a chance to bless because humans are involved in its creation. No matter where one works within a large educational system, there is an obligation to humanize one's act. We may not bring the system to its knees, and, in fact, that may not be a worthy goal, but to fulfil our role imaginatively is to give to the system a surplus it does not ask and cannot cause by itself. Even if we feel that our piece of the system is a tiny eddy of no apparent influence, on behalf of the students at its mercy we must try to give the best of our humanity to our act. Artificial systems should not reduce our humanity to a parody of itself. We made these systems, we are their masters, and we should continue to pour our humanity into them relentlessly at every point, and if they burst, metamorphose or short-circuit, then so be it. It wouldn't be the first time wineskins have split.

When we created the HSC English 'Extension 1' examination paper in 2008, we based it on artistic assemblages by and in the spirit of American artist Joseph Cornell. We presented students in each elective with an image of one of his assemblages that suited the elective, or an image of an assemblage created by us that was inspired by him. We were offering students of literature, in love and respect, the best of ourselves. We were giving them a gift of our (and Cornell's) imagination to provoke their imaginative responses to literary texts all within the confines of what some would see as the most oppressive cell of formal education, the exam room. There in the tightest spot, the cramped vertex of syllabus and student, we gave the possibility of multiplicity. Students could select a single element from the assemblage's multiplicity, or imaginatively cohere a personal story from the components within the assemblage that spoke to them. A head teacher at a school full of students who struggle academically said how this paper invited those students in and let them speak to their elective from their own experience in a way that enabled them to excel. Another teacher said this paper generated some of the most extraordinary responses he had read in thirty years.

It came down to one thing: not dissing the system, but blessing it. Blessing according to our humanity and care. Not taking revenge on revenge effects. Giving more than reacting. Shaking the superflux, as King Lear might say (3.4.35). We should not underestimate the power of love and aesthetics to permeate and transform structures according to their own energy flows once we release them. We should not think we have to dismantle a structure in the same way it was built. Far better to release joy and beauty into it – let them do the work. If we built a system by reason and it became a rod for our backs, why turn to reason to ease our pain?

2006: Collateral damage

'Positive turbulence,' to borrow Stan Gryskiewicz's term, comes in many forms.[2] It is much needed in these times of *de rigueur* equilibrium where all learning must be foreknown and micro-measured.

In 2006 I got hit by a wallaby. In twenty years of bushwalking in Ku-ring-gai Chase National Park I'd seen countless wallabies which are the 'native burghers' there in the north of Sydney.[3] They are Swamp Wallabies and their home is creek- and river-washed coastal bushland. The vegetation is dense and tough, with spots of more open woodland. Native grasses, hakeas and grevilleas, endless wattles, eucalypts and angophoras, are all tossed through with cream-and-orange caves, rocky bluffs and tessellated pavements of Sydney sandstone. Thousands of Aboriginal rock engravings of wallabies and whales, echidnas and fish, deities and mortals, prick the whole fabric like stitches tying it to Dreamtime.

The swampies are adorable, gentle creatures, smaller than the iconic kangaroo, and with coarse fur that is a mix of bark-grey and brown, except the tail which is lush chocolate tending to black. Their warm animal smell lingers in the scrub, mixing with the aromas of the Australian bush in a subtle, natural concoction I can now, blessedly, never forget.

Encountered by the bushwalker, swampies never stay, but hop away, their pace measured by the unique iambic pentameter of crunching undergrowth preceded by the nothingness of flight: – crash, – crash, – crash, – crash, – crash. I cannot express how I love them. Nor my gratitude to my dad for initiating me as a child into the ways of Ku-ring-gai Chase, where we used to sit and watch the Wedge-Tailed Eagles soar from which I took my middle name.

A long rolling road to West Head Lookout stretches through the national park and as an adult cyclist it became a training route for me. In 2006 I was descending one of the dips at 60 kilometres per hour, my training partner on his bike 30 metres behind me. Without warning a dark blur materialized under my left elbow. A split-second later my bike shunted sideways and my feet popped from their cleats. I glanced to the left as I steadied the decelerating bike and saw a swampy roll backwards from the collision, right himself, and hop away into the bush, – crash, – crash, – crash.

He'd smacked my left leg and the vertical centre post below my seat. Smacked hard. A smudge of wallaby fur blended with my own hair on my calf, and tufts protruded from the Velcro strap that still held my pump to the bike's frame. I coasted to the side of the road and stopped, adrenalin surging. I was lucky not to be sprawled on the road. My partner arrived, his eyes wide like plates.

'Did you see that?' I asked.

'He waited for you,' Brian said. 'I was watching him. He just sat by the side of the road until we got to him. I thought we'd go right by him. Then as soon as you got near, he went. I couldn't believe it.'

Setting the more positive feelings aside – because I felt honoured by the collision, by physical contact at last with soul-mates who never dared let me get close till now – we had a problem. The impact had ruptured my rear wheel. The rim was split between three spokes.

Why did the wallaby cross the road? In the absence of explanation from Swampy himself, Shakespeare offered commentary. It irked me, as it 'irks' Duke Senior in *As You Like It*, that such 'poor dappled fools . . . Should in their own confines' (2.1.21–4) be harmed by our intrusion. We were miles from home. This was Swampy's world. As a road cyclist, I was focused on executing a technical and relatively meaningless activity, riding from A to B and back again, piercing through another world and making it mere scenery to my achievement. He'd buckled my system, brought me to a halt, and forced me to reconsider my way home.

Like the makers of West Head Road, literary educators carve a path through the natural scrubland of literature to enable student knowledge and appreciation of its qualities and value. Teachers and academics can become too technical and tunnel-visioned in their ways, executing procedures that merely endorse disciplinary systems with increasingly detailed particularity. They are like well-drilled cyclists who initially train on park roads because of their beauty, and yet, ironically, as time passes, their incomprehension grows about the meaning of their context. It is possible to teach Literary Studies and forget both literature and learning.

Why did Swampy cross the road? To teach the teacher that systems have casualties. That systems are arbitrary intrusions. That systems give comfort and feel natural, but not always, and not to all. That even while they envelop like a mother, violation is their middle name. To teach me that living things need to, and always have the capacity to, inject turbulence into systems. To show me that such impulsive, ill-considered or strategic reactions are necessary crises. Crises for the system, the teacher, and perhaps most acutely, the student.

2007: **System transition**

For nearly a decade I taught first-year university courses while simultaneously working with the NSW Board of Studies. I saw what students write in first-year literature assessment tasks at university and what they are trained to write in Year 12 literature assessment tasks. I saw what they are rewarded for at school and what they are penalized for at university: often the two are the same. I saw what teachers have to care about and I saw what academics have to care about: worlds apart at one level, yet also one world. I realized that the academic is not good and the teacher bad: they are the same. I realized that the schools are not bad and the universities good: they are the same. We are all fragile humans doing the best we can with our love of literature and teaching – in a sea of strong currents that pull us round and push us here and there. These currents are a volatile mixture of the visible and unseen, institutional and personal, forceful and gentle.

In less than six months after their final school exams, thousands of Australian students submit their first pieces of written work for assessment within English courses at university. Shortly after that, for a proportion of students, the dismal grade on their first assignment will leave them dumbstruck. The outward signs vary. Some are angry, some dismissive (read hurt), others puzzled and some submissive (read pragmatic). A whispered phrase heard around April or May as junior university students drift through the corridors with returned essays in hand is: 'I've *never* had a *mark* like *this* before!'

In Australia we do not teach 'First Year Composition' to university juniors in any comprehensive way: students can specialize early and tend to 'learn on the job' within discipline areas. Junior modules at my university tend to incorporate a small amount of discipline-focused, workshop guidance in essay composition and, where necessary, students can access a range of writing courses and workshops offered by other parts of the university such as The Writing Hub, the Write Site and the Learning Centre.

It's not just the mark; though of course a mark in the 50–60 percentile for a student whose school English assignments always scored in the top performance band feels like collision with an unseen iceberg. These high achievers are shocked to find academic markers' comments reducing their grammar, style, literary analysis, composition of argument and engagement with secondary material to rubble. To compound matters, the student then finds the marker's comments curiously difficult to apply effectively to the writing of the next assignment. Another disheartening grade may follow and, inexplicably, the marker's comments on that piece appear to advise the same improvements as before.

The student wonders: Am I stupid? Have I always been stupid and my school teachers hid it from me? I don't get it.

Generally speaking, the first-year literature students who fail to comprehend *how* the essays they produce fail to deliver what is required of them somehow thrash their way to shore. They arrive dripping at the end of semester with a bare 'Pass' and may repeat the inelegant procedure the next semester. It ain't pretty, but they do get through and over subsequent semesters their research, grammar, style and essay writing skills in many cases mysteriously improve. More in spite of the system, than due to it. Not uncommonly, some of them go on to excel in Literary Studies and even enter academia. Swampy finally got through; he took a few more hits to the head, but he's an Associate Professor now. What is going on?

We tend to treat Year 12 students as one thing and first-year university students as another. We imagine that one year has passed since the student was at school and that his or her intellectual framework for acquisition, arrangement and delivery of academic knowledge has evolved in that time. No such things have occurred. We might think that school teachers and academics in English departments are, as it were, teaching from the same textbook with the same glossary of technical terms, but this too is erroneous.

The fact is that the Year 12 student and the first-semester university student are one and the same person. They are not distinct entities; they are not even the one entity at different moments. They are the same entity at the same moment – a mere three months later, with no additional formal education in between. We need broader ways of thinking about these students so that we are not locked into understanding them always according to discontinuous and self-perpetuating systems such as 'school student' and 'university junior.' The broader category – such as 'teenager formally studying English' – may help us realize that the one individual has been deeply drilled (consciously and unconsciously) in the methods and ideals of one pedagogical system (secondary school) and then finds him- or herself in the grip of a different system (the university). Each system enjoys unquestioned authority over the student. Broadly shared or superficially visible common-alities in the teaching of literature in Australian schools and universities do exist, but when it comes down to it, first-year essays reveal that schools and universities teach and reward students of English literature in some markedly different ways.

We need to care for our teenagers a little more than our systems. Transition abounds with revenge effects. At present, first-semester university students are invisibly penalized for not being what they were not made. The finely honed skills, vocabulary and methods that were rewarded in Year 12 suddenly become deficits in first-year essays. White is black and black is white. Known terms and methods turn out to be unknown, misunderstood or misapplied.

It is all too easy for academics to mark first-year essays, which frequently are Year 12 essays with blind attempts at value-adding, against an ideal exemplified in second-year work. This can draw students forward toward production of work of higher quality, but academics teaching first year also need to be aware that they are engaged in a colonizing project. This project requires no less than submission of the student mind to a paradigm of pedagogy and scholarship that from the student's perspective comes out of the blue (even where it may initially feel familiar) and is often directly contrary to the student's reasonable expectations. The student is not stupid, but is actually working double-time to comprehend the marker's comments, terminology and imperatives which arise from an alien paradigm of scholarship and cause confusion when interpreted according to the student's previously internalized paradigm. Hence the academic's repetition of advice is caused by the student's unwitting misapplication of it.

For the student it is particularly disturbing that the parameters of what an essay is and does, and how it may organize itself and conduct its argument, all seem to have changed. And this is to say nothing of the profound change in the modes of information delivery to students when they enter university or the fundamental shift in the ideological and pedagogical expectations placed on them as literature students. No wonder it can take a year or more for students to work out how to write essays that impress academics. The intellectual hurdles that students deal with are not primarily to do with enhanced comprehension of the subject matter, but rather more to do with systemic adjustment. It is in fact extraordinary how well they do given they are learning and baffled on so many fronts at once. They are learning the system, the subject area and their system subjecthood all at once, and if this weren't cognitive load enough, almost none of this is ever adequately or explicitly contrasted by their lecturers with the versions they knew at school and carry in their head.

This is because the incomprehension goes both ways. Many academics are illiterate in the language of Year 12 student learning and fail to comprehend the principles the first-year student is attempting to showcase. The colonizing academic is not the one who is required to change and has little motivation to learn idiosyncratic HSC terminology such as 'composer,' 'responder,' 'technique' and 'textual integrity' (which is nothing like what an academic might think!). Many students don't realize that paraphrase at school may constitute plagiarism at university. Many don't know the difference between assertion and demonstration. Some think that large words and general concepts are just what academics want to read and they have trouble comprehending the academic push for smaller words, shorter sentences and fewer generalizations. Once praised above their peers for seeing the big picture, students are now criticized for such presumption.

School teachers and academics are flat-out attempting to meet the requirements of the particular educational system in which they are embedded without trying to deal with the task of secondary–tertiary dialogue and collaboration. Yet the current climate will force us to seek refuge in mutual understanding. We need to believe that teachers and academics are united in the same profession and thence to share wisdom with each other on how best to give.

2008: Ardenspace

In the HSC syllabus, the study of *As You Like It* is bound inextricably to the notion of 'belonging.' Many students front up at the final exam either actually believing or pretending to believe that the theme of 'belonging' somehow inherently belongs to *As You Like It*. The system thus speaks to itself through the play and the students. What if we asked the play to speak back to the system?

This is worth doing because in *As You Like It* Shakespeare unveils learning systems and models positive turbulence for us. The play may be seen as a theatrical metaphor for pedagogical practice in Literary Studies. It offers three distinct spaces – the usurping court of Duke Frederick, the exiled court of his brother Duke Senior or Ferdinand, and the Forest of Arden – and displays varied scenes of human ignorance, learning and creativity within them. The two courts may be seen as extremes on a linear scale that measures the quantum of liberty in any space of learning. The third space, the forest, signifies innovation and while not on the linear scale is intimately related to it.

The authoritarian voice of Duke Frederick roars through the first space like the bellow of a pedagogue whose arbitrary commands are driven by fears of loss of authority. The 'humorous Duke' (2.3.8) stands for the teacher whose methods tend toward control and constraint. The intellectual content of the classroom is his gift to give and he gives it in strict conformity to curriculum laws. Many excellent teachers operate this way, preparing syllabus-aligned content and objectives of classes in great detail and herding students through pre-built intellectual pens and conduits in which they are nourished and catch sight of inspiring, pre-designated vistas. It is predominantly a one-way transmission model of teaching and the students are given little room for extensive freedom of thought. Teacher Frederick's method presupposes students as relatively passive and he fundamentally (but not necessarily consciously) distrusts their ability and desire to learn. In Biggs and Tang's terms (40–5), he creates a 'Theory X' pedagogical climate.

Ferdinand's exiled court operates on decidedly different principles. Hierarchy is preserved, yet he is open to learning new ideas from his companions and from his own reflections on process and context. He resembles the teacher who deploys a pluralized teaching and learning praxis in which students are encouraged to contribute genuinely to exploratory conversations. Teacher Ferdinand's method presupposes students as relatively active and he fundamentally trusts their ability and desire to learn. He creates a 'Theory Y' pedagogical climate. Teacher Ferdinand tends to promote creative interactivity and discovery over transmission and internalization of pre-determined skills and knowledge, while Teacher Frederick promotes the reverse. The former is open and risky, the latter closed and secure. Educational theorists rightly argue the desirability of achieving some mean between these 'X' and 'Y' extremes.[4]

All educational 'courts,' regardless of where they may lie on the scale, impose a paradigm on reality and thus are purveyors of convention or 'usurpers': both Frederick and Ferdinand are identified in the play as usurpers of natural rights (2.1.27–8). The scene of learning in schools and universities is inherently 'usurped' because natural powers of knowledge acquisition and creativity are coerced into regularized protocols so as to produce arrangements of knowledge that are recognizable to, and measurable as outcomes within, artificial systems.

A virtue of Teacher Ferdinand's classroom is that it is more likely to encourage double-loop thinking than his brother's which entrenches single-loop. Single-loop thought is defined by W. R. Ashby and elaborated by Chris Argyris and Donald A. Schön in relation to their paradigm of 'Model I' and 'Model II' learning.[5] To employ Ashby's metaphor, single-loop thinking resembles the behaviour of a thermostat in a household heating system: it detects a problem (a drop in room temperature below the pre-set mark), activates a response to rectify it (increases the flow of hot water), and ceases the response when the room temperature has risen to the required level. This oscillating process occurs within pre-established operating principles or settings and does not alter them: rather, all actions occurring are reactions seeking to 'satisfice' or maintain the governing principles.[6]

In contrast, Ashby likens double-loop thinking to the intervention of the householder to change the thermostat's setting which is to alter a governing variable with the effect that lower order processes must fall into line with the new setting. Thus in single-loop learning 'we learn to maintain the field of constancy' while in double-loop 'we learn to change the field of constancy.'[7] Both types are essential: single-loop enables us to deal with mundane or repetitive tasks that require little thought, while double-loop enables us to query governing variables so as to address complex problems and effect significant innovation.[8]

It is easy to see how the HSC system described can push its human subjects toward single-loop learning. Single-loop learning is also exemplified in the way university lecturers in

English detect specific deficits in first-year student skills and subject knowledge and create new learning tasks or modules to restore the deficits. This is thermostatic behaviour that remains within the governing variables of tertiary learning, but does not query them. A double-loop response to the same perception of deficit might include the collaborative reconsideration of the teaching and learning package being delivered to students in senior-high and junior-university. Such a response has the potential to effect changes in the field of constancy that will lead to modified processes at sublevels. It is salutary to consider that both educators and their students can be guilty of too little double-loop thought. Academics may accuse first-year students of single-loop narrow-mindedness in approaching the interpretation of texts, while they themselves continue hammering away at single-loop solutions to this very problem.

Key questions arise from this. Given the youth of students in senior-high and the early stage of their intellectual progression through bodies of subject-area knowledge, to what degree is it advisable that they engage in double-loop learning activities? Is the university rather than the high school the better place for such activities given the need for some accrual of fundamentals? Even if it is, and this is not necessarily so, to what degree should school students be alerted to the possibility and value of double-loop learning? Given the foregoing discussion of the HSC, it would be dishonest to think that merely alerting students is enough; the formal system would need to validate and reward this sort of paradigm-querying learning in robust ways. And to what degree do universities promote double-loop thinking?[9] Surely we have a lot to gain from teachers and academics collaboratively asking: what sort of learners are we making and how can we engage in double-loop consideration of how we might make them differently and better?

Argyris and Schön embed single- and double-loop learning within their two models of how individuals function as actors in organizations. If we think of the two dukes in *As You Like*

It as managers, Duke Frederick aligns most closely with Argyris and Schön's 'Model I,' while Duke Ferdinand exemplifies 'Model II.'[10] The 'Model I' manager takes command of situations unilaterally, controlling the definition of the problem and tasks, censoring information, ignoring the human impact of his actions and assigning blame. Duke Frederick's court is characterized by autocratic fiats, threats and secret meetings. The duke plunges ever deeper into single-loop reactions that escalate in urgency and fury as he strives to maintain the field of constancy. His unimaginative mind can only process Rosalind in the plane of his political ambition, and underlying this is his fear that she is intellectually 'too subtle' and unpredictable a thinker for him to manage (1.3.74–9).

In contrast, the governing variables of Argyris and Schön's 'Model II' manager include maximizing valid information so that individuals can make informed choices for themselves. The manager is a collaborator and is open to productive debate of opposing viewpoints. Processes are subject to public testing and correction, and double-loop learning is propagated.[11] The exiled Ferdinand uses his adversity to trigger double-loop learning that re-evaluates and potentially disconfirms his previously held governing variables. He discovers a 'life more sweet' than the old life and a deeper self-knowledge that is also outward looking (2.1.1–69; 2.7.88–204). He values un-coerced human expression (2.1.27–8; 2.2.67–8; 2.7.140–67) and the unexpected (2.7.103–40; 4.3.141–3; 5.4.145–6, 174–7, 195–6). Like any double-loop thinker or 'Model II' manager, he is able to love the alien.

Taken together, the tensions embodied in the two courts – between constraint and liberty, transmission and discovery, unilateralism and collaboration – feature in all formal learning spaces as educators negotiate relations between system, subject and student to achieve best practice. The third conceptual space in the play, the Forest of Arden, does not lie on the same continuum, but does have concrete effects there. It is a space that is imaginable by those on the continuum, although such imagining is hard if one's habits of mind are formed by a 'Theory X' or 'Model I' context.

The forest is inherently sportive, multivalent and provisional. Credible realities, planned meetings, known characters and unfolding plots are woven through a less obviously directed fabric of pastoral romance and social satire, emblematic tableau and miraculous transformation, and linguistic and gender deconstruction. The audience witnesses a series of seemingly random encounters between characters whose verbal exchanges loosen inherited meanings and multiply viewpoints. For the characters this amounts to positive turbulence at a cognitive level. To go into the forest is to have its turbulence go into you.

If there is a constant in the forest, it is the power of *if* which pervades its ontology and epistemology like a vital force. To enter the magic 'circle of this forest' (5.4.34), as Frederick, Oliver and Orlando discover, is to enter a zone hostile to single-loop thinking and the routine satisficing of fields of constancy. Oliver and Frederick are converted via personal experience outside their normal zone of operation and their transformations contribute to changes in characters such as Jaques (5.4.178–83), Celia (5.2.1–12), Ferdinand (5.4.161–3) and Orlando (5.2.9–12). Oliver and Frederick are no longer what they were and are now able to embrace the alien – the former literally marrying 'Aliena' (5.2.5–12, 62) and the latter adopting 'a religious life' (5.4.178–80).

In a butterfly effect of transformation, amplifying feedback loops of change pass between sporadically interacting characters. This fertile mixture of regularity and irregularity suggests a 'complex adaptive system,'[12] yet the term 'system' seems inapt to describe the interactivity of the forest. The forest presents 'complex responsive processes of relating' rather than any predetermined system.[13] It operates in a state that is 'far-from-equilibrium' or 'on the edge of chaos.'[14] This state – lying beyond the 'canalized' or 'locked-in'[15] processes of Frederick's court, and even beyond the freer intercommunications of Ferdinand's court – exists on the brink of randomness and thus possesses the greatest process complexity and the greatest likelihood of fostering the emergence of the new within individuals and collectives. When characters commit to practices of mobile connectivity on 'the edge of chaos' their canalized mental habits – such as Orlando's Petrarchan understanding of love or Frederick's autocratic rule – that served them well in satisfying other systems, break down, and authentic creativity is enabled.[16] That which 'emerges' is thus not fully owned, nor fully directed or caused by any single participating entity, but is an outcome of the complex interactivity itself.[17] Such emergent novelty or pattern is the judgment of the forest.

The language of *if* pervades the play, especially the forest scenes, but is densest around Rosalind who incarnates the principle of possibility. Rosalind is a magical 'boy' and a boy actor, 'forest-born' and 'a magician' (5.4.30, 5.2.69, Epilogue). Her relentless double-loop thinking facilitates a positive unsettling of other characters' assumptions (5.2.50–71, 99–117; 5.4.1–25). She is Rosalind playing 'Ganymede' to empower herself in the forest, where she is also, more complexly, Rosalind playing 'Ganymede' playing 'Rosalind' to empower Orlando. She devotes considerable energy to destabilizing Orlando's expectations and habits of thought so that they balance on the edge of chaos without being driven into a completely hectic state where no useful cognitive order could result. Her 'education of Orlando,' to borrow a phrase from Marjorie Garber's excellent account,[18] relies on involving him in complex responsive processes of relating in order to facilitate the emergence of new ways of thinking.

In the final scenes, a linguistic architecture of sound emerges from balanced arrays of *if*-clauses delivered by different characters: 'If this be so,' 'If there be truth in sight,' 'If you be not he' (5.2.99–101; 5.4.116–22). The aural patterning hints toward the promised, but yet unseen, order that the characters are committing themselves to by their words. As Maura Slattery Kuhn observes, *if* is the 'springboard' via which characters signal faith in the 'unreal' premises of the forest and thereby launch themselves toward a fulfilment beyond their expectations.[19] The dénouement is deferred by an intervening conversation between Touchstone and Jaques that affirms the power of *if* to achieve resolution: '"if" is the only peacemaker; much virtue in "if"' (5.4.100–1). Hymen suddenly appears and presides over a recognition scene permeated by *if*s realized, but as Valerie Traub notes, '[e]ven Hymen's mandate is qualified' by *if*: 'If truth holds true contents.'[20]

The Forest of Arden is a space of complex responsive processes of relating. Emergence is enabled by a commitment to *if*-promises, statement of *if*-theories, living in *if*-states, embracing *if*-transformations. These ultimately materialize as a new order of reality. But this new order will not settle. Rosalind is the most alert contributor to the forest's 'bounded or limited instability,'[21] its complexity and creativity, and her refusal to relinquish *if,* even in the Epilogue ('If I were a woman'), illustrates the beneficial uncontainability or ripple effect of what we might call 'ardenspace.' Traub and other critics emphasize the importance of Rosalind's Epilogue to the play's resistance to and dissolution of inherited categories.[22] The 'entire logic' of the play, Traub writes, 'works against. . .fixing upon and reifying any one mode of desire.'[23] *If* exemplifies commitment to an entirely experimental state.

Ardenspace actualizes such experimentation. If the courts of Frederick and Ferdinand represent forms of institutional learning, the Forest of Arden is the archetype of ardenspace. An ardenspace is a space of pedagogical exploration beyond the formal systems that promotes complex responsive interactivity in anticipation of emergence. It is essentially an 'exile' space because it lies outside, yet in relation to, conventional educational 'courts.' It offers a zone between system and asystem, lived and imagined, that is conducive to double-loop thinking, positive turbulence and emergence.

The exiles might include teachers, academics and students, but also other less predictable participants. The locations might include school and university campuses, but also other less predictable places. Here at 'the edge of chaos' participants

welcome the unexpected and look for the emergence of innovative ideas that may be actualized within and beyond established educational infrastructures. We must create ardenspaces,
the more numerous and diverse the better, so that innovative
(or 'exilic') ideas can flow into iterative (or 'usurped') systems.
And to these ardenspaces, to the mysterious life and judgment
of the forest, we must become, if only temporarily, 'foolish
runaways' (2.2.21).

Ardenspace

CHAPTER THREE

Shakespeare Reloaded
(Life at the system edge)

2007: Ardenspace meets Linkagespace

Ardenspace is a type of dreaming. It is a space of creative interactivity for temporary exiles of educational courts. It is creativity provoked by system. It is not, *per se*, a revolution, or an all-out assault on system by its malcontents. It is participatory storytelling in response to, about, from and against system. It is transgressive in respect to systems, categories and habits, but more importantly, it is free, generative and metamorphic. It goes some way to manifesting Agamben's idea of study as serious play decoupled from instrumentalism.[1] It conjures unpredicted emergence and sends positive turbulence through people and systems. It wrong-foots system and hotwires system's agents. It is voluntary yet necessary, personal yet communal, ephemeral yet ramifying. Its vitality, flow and humanity remind us that system has not always been and that its limits can be felt out, explored, critiqued. More than this, ardenspace (so far as it can) allows speech beyond system, a non-systemic sharing that remains in sight of system and ultimately pours poetry back into pedagogy.

What might ardenspaces look like in Literary Studies? There are, presumably, many ways to actualize an ardenspace.

It begins by seeing systems. If we weren't system builders we wouldn't need ardenspaces. System gives ardenspace meaning and value: all the more so now as rococo systems proliferate through institutional education. Ardenspaces, therefore, involve negotiation with systems and formal courts because we are systems' agents: they own our time, they demand explanations, they restrict our activity and thought, and they have enabling mechanisms we can exploit.

Without actualization, ardenspace remains a phantom unworthy of the name. All system creatures have their complaints and fantasies – profound, trivial, contradictory, emotive, rational, fleeting, recurrent – which are usually normalized as the system grind of a professional career in education. They are a chaos of discontinuous affect, venting and counter-logics that never cohere into complexes of any transformative power. Ardenspace is different because in it the moving shadows, the spurts of affect and desire, all become something.

In 2007, with these ideas on my mind, I turned to the Australian Research Council's Linkage Project funding scheme to enable ardenspace. I needed systems to speak to systems. I came to think of this ARC mechanism as 'linkage-space.' Linkagespace is not essential to the causation of ardenspace. It was simply a path presented to me by the system and I took it. Linkagespace is thoroughly infrastructural, an off-the-shelf system interface requiring submission to fine-grained rules. In my view, I would become obedient to linkage-space to enable the disobedience of ardenspace.

Linkagespace is a bureaucratic construct, a corporate protocol fuelled by pro formas. The Linkage Grants scheme sets up a formal research agreement and funding pool between the university and the non-tertiary PO. It locks you into codependency and certain types of non-traditional tertiary outputs. It hazes you with a maelstrom of paperwork and para-research: progress reports, appointment forms, ethics forms, media releases, translating documents between organizations, obtaining signatures, explaining oneself, persuading boards and groups, doing interviews and marketing. It drives you into the strange world of humanities academics whose mouths are sulfurous with commercial language such as: 'find someone with money,' 'who are the stakeholders?,' 'what do they want?,' 'cut a deal,' 'lawyers,' 'value-add,' 'negotiate' and 'win-win.'

Here's a causal line. Universities are overtly pressuring their staff to win external grant funding. To win a competitive grant is a meritorious deed: it brings credit and reward not just to the individual system creature but to the institution enveloping that creature. Grant success has the added benefit of enhancing the quantity of one's research output and this secures one's sabbatical and guards against losing one's job. Linkage Project grant applications are statistically twice as likely to be successful as Discovery Project applications, but Linkage Projects are more than double the work to create, negotiate and manage. In other words, the reason for humanities academics initially (and perhaps recurrently) giving it a go are primarily (not always) system reasons, not research reasons. Neoliberalism is contributing its shaping power to humanities research, forcing us and our disciplines to be and become in ways we may not have chosen unprompted.

2007: Seeing Rosalind

When I first considered creating a Linkage Project I thought, grandly and unrealistically, of uniting Literary Studies and some large corporation like IBM or Macquarie Group. I soon realized that my approach was all wrong: it was a system approach, mechanical and soulless.

I retreated to my heart and asked two professional questions: (1) what do I love? and (2) who shares that love? This was my breakthrough. The first answer was 'literature and teaching.' The second answer was 'a school.' I would begin where I was, within my devoted marriage to literary art and its analysis, rather than with a marriage of convenience to a business. Nonetheless, this decision still constituted a type of infidelity to the standard model of literature research at university, but at least truth lay at its core.

It was revealing that my first thoughts had been purely system thoughts (find a cashed-up company and make hay together) and only secondarily had I valued what I actually do value (literature and teaching). The move from first to second thoughts was a crucial moment of release when my thoughts began to displace or colonize system thoughts (I do not say there is full separation). I contacted a friend, Shauna, with whom I'd worked at the Board of Studies. She was an English teacher and Head of Curriculum at Barker College, an independent Anglican school on Sydney's North Shore. Barker College has 2,000 students, an English department the same size as ours at Sydney University (about thirty staff), and a deep investment in the study and performance of Shakespeare.

The school was ideally placed for a research partnership to explore Shakespeare pedagogy – but it was not the school in the abstract that drew me. It was Shauna. She was a teacher who lived the virtue in *if* – in her own learning, in fuelling her students' learning, in imagining alternative structures. She possessed a disturbing blend of relentless positivity, creative intelligence and pragmatic system knowledge. New ideas stuck to her and sparkled. When they fell off and grew into perverse little monsters she knew how to handle them.

To me she was Rosalind: someone who could lead others out of formal courts of learning and into exile. She represented how linkagespace could be called on to enable ardenspace. If we believed, if we were careful, we would be in touch with magic 'most profound. . .and yet not damnable' (*As You Like It*, 5.2.57–60). We could do some good.

To some of my colleagues she was the Dark Lady: someone who pedalled corporate aims and would be the conduit of private dealing between the university and an elite school. She represented privilege and would 'corrupt my saint [Literary Studies] to be a devil, / Wooing his purity with her foul pride' (Sonnet 144). She was my 'worser spirit' seeking to 'win me soon to hell' (Sonnet 144) by drawing me into a project that would weaken the intellectual rigour of my research and set a precedent for subordinating research directions to stakeholder directives.

We assembled two teams to collaborate on the creation of 'Shakespeare Reloaded' as a Linkage Project grant application: at Barker, the Headmaster Dr Rod Kefford, Shauna and the Heads of English and Drama; and at Sydney University, Professor Penny Gay, Dr Kate Flaherty and me. Our aim was to use the linkagespace as a mechanism for enacting an ardenspace within which we could explore Shakespeare pedagogy at school and university. We wanted to see how the formal educational systems worked and to understand how and where and to what ends human creativity might flourish therein.

We had two crucial premises: academics and school teachers are entirely equal as literary professionals; and, an attempt to *understand* the current situation in secondary and tertiary Literary Studies was a valid, indeed essential, object of this collaborative research, before any precipitous rush into fabricating supposed *solutions*. If after three years we had done no more than consolidate a genuine relationship based on professional equality across our related sectors and gained some traction on how to articulate the problems facing us, I would be more than happy. These are not solutions *per se*, but worthy goals. However, I could see how the tertiary research climate enveloping me would likely read this methodology: a project that makes 'slow' progress a virtue and consciously values 'personal' and 'exclusive' connection to a PO is not a project that will automatically fit our sector's fast research cycles, standardized publication outputs and affect-purged discourses. And it certainly won't boost our low-socioeconomic enrolments.

That said, the grant application was successful and the three-year project began in 2008. Despite the critics and my own anxieties, I knew that this was more than a callous win-win deal where the school could trade on association with our university's name and expertise and I could draw external funding into the faculty. I knew because I knew the people involved and the integrity of the project design. Maybe the system spoke first, maybe it caused me (in some significant ways) to cause this, but without doubt we were gaming it our way. We were doing it for Swampy.

2008–10: Shakespeare Reloaded

'Shakespeare Reloaded' was designed as a cluster of distinct yet interconnected research and teaching components. Four key components were: an academic-in-residence program; a travel fellowship scheme; a conference; and the teaching of two postgraduate Shakespeare modules on site at the school. The idea was that these components would facilitate distinct approaches to the exploration of Shakespeare pedagogy and that they would have differing and partially overlapping memberships. In addition to these components which were co-produced by teachers and academics, and sometimes co-produced by students, the academic team also pursued individual research projects. I was researching transition studies and systems of learning; my PhD student Linzy Brady was researching teachers' professional learning within collaborative Shakespeare projects; Penny Gay was researching postmodern performance and learning; and Kate Flaherty was researching Australasian Shakespeare performance and pedagogy through the ages.

'Shakespeare Reloaded' was a complex system by virtue of being a loosely assembled array of disparate approaches to the same research theme. Participants enjoyed varied levels of involvement in varied aspects of the project – not all wanted to attain an MA or Graduate Certificate; not all could be travel fellows; not all felt able to speak at the conference – and they shared their distinct and overlapping experiences with each other informally and in workshops at the school. Thus, we created numerous spaces in which to consider how

Shakespeare pedagogy was occurring. Within these spaces and across them we repeatedly asked: 'what if?' We sought to facilitate the emergence of innovations in pedagogy and transformations of teachers, academics and students by lively exchanges of ideas. There was a lot going on in 'Shakespeare Reloaded' so what follows is just a taste of it.[2]

The academic-in-residence program was the crucial mechanism by which we built cordial and knowledgeable relationships between academics and teachers. It meant that for at least two days in every school term the academic team visited the school and collaborated with teachers on experimental teaching and learning activities, lectures and workshops for students and staff, and planning meetings. This component had maximum buy-in from the school community, continued for the duration of the project (2008–10), and generated teaching resources that were trialled at Barker and made available to NSW teachers via publication.

We gave lectures to school staff on academic themes such as early modern understandings of the self, philosophical contexts for *Hamlet*, and the debate around Shakespeare as a writer for print and/or stage. We had small-scale 'conversations' between teachers and academics using discussion sheets on topics such as: *The Tempest*'s emotional topography; *Othello* and comedy; and *Lear* according to Wu Hsing-Kuo's Taiwanese adaptation *Lear is Here*. We talked to Year 10 students about teenager-hood in early modernity and *Romeo and Juliet*; played a newly-devised game with senior students studying *Richard III* to reveal Richard's strategies of human interaction and contingency control; and experimented with various essay composition workshops. Teachers ran focus groups with students to get feedback on events and participated as active researchers within their own classrooms and as case-study subjects for Linzy's doctoral research. We had mini-conferences where teachers presented innovative pedagogical approaches to each other.[3]

The academic-in-residence program occasionally dovetailed with the school's professional development (PD) program.

Teachers often feel PD is autocratic, onerous and predictable with the result that they remain unengaged and unchanged. 'Shakespeare Reloaded' was helpful in offering PD for exiles in an ardenspace of collaborative learning, rather than bureaucratic PD for captive courtiers. One teacher wrote, 'I love the idea of bringing the different perspectives on teaching and learning from university and school together and allowing each to inform the practice of the other.' Another confessed to 'never having studied Shakespeare at university, or even beyond Year 9 when I was at school, so it was great just being able to deepen my understanding of Shakespeare so that I can teach it better.'

Teachers and academics need to experience professional conversations stripped of the rhetorics of competition, defensiveness and prejudgment and characterized by deep interest in everyone's professional experiences. Such conversations are facilitated by the establishment of long-term relationships between specific schools and specific universities and authentic, self-reflective, collaborative ventures. Unexpectedly, as the teachers and academics fled into the exile spaces of our project events they discovered that the intellectual vitality they experienced worked to unblock hitherto clogged communication flows between colleagues who normally saw each other every day. This was positive turbulence as flushing and descaling.

The annual travel fellowship scheme was at the other end of the scale: it paired one teacher with one academic and sent them on an intellectual and geographical journey together to Shakespeare-related research, teaching and cultural sites overseas. This liberated the teacher from the daily grind of school and gave him or her international professional experience. It blended friendship-building with a sharing of the distinct professional responses of two educators to the same Shakespeare stimuli. On return to Australia the pair shared their experiences with colleagues via workshops, new initiatives and informal conversations.

In 2008 the travel fellow was English teacher Lucy Solomon who visited the Oregon Shakespeare Festival in Ashland with academic Kate Flaherty. She brought back to her school resources and enthusiasm to create an engaging introduction to Shakespeare's plays for Year 7 students – something the school had not attempted before and now succeeded in implementing. Her ten-week scheme of work was called 'Shakespeare's Theatre: Weird Words or Bloody Battles?' It was an introductory study of key Shakespearean speeches designed to foster a sense of Shakespeare as fun, exciting and accessible. It was based on speeches from *Macbeth, Midsummer Night's Dream, Tempest, As You Like It* and *Hamlet*. Students were required to research and create a poster about Shakespeare's life and theatrical context and analyse speeches as text and drama. They had to create a news advertisement for a Shakespeare play which included performance information and their original translations of lines from a speech. The scheme of work included internet and film resources and ended with a showcase of work and an Elizabethan Feast. The fellowship changed what Lucy thought was possible for Year 7 and gave her the impetus to cause curriculum change in her school.

The third component was a conference on Shakespeare and pedagogy co-hosted by the 'Shakespeare Reloaded' project and the Australian and New Zealand Shakespeare Association, with papers delivered by teachers and academics on site at the University of Sydney and Barker College. This was a brilliant opportunity for school teachers and academics to speak with equal authority about how Shakespeare is taught and learned rather than letting academics dominate the agenda.[4]

The fourth component was the teaching of two of the university's postgraduate modules ('Shakespeare and the Renaissance' and 'Shakespeare and Modernity') on site at Barker College in the Northern Suburbs rather than on the main university campus in central Sydney. This enabled busy teachers at various schools in that area of Sydney to enrol as postgraduate students because they could now study closer to home and work. A distinctive feature of this element of 'Shakespeare Reloaded' was the transformation of teachers into students, many not having studied formally let alone composed assessable essays for over twenty years. The Headmaster, leading by example, was one of the students. The assessment scheme for the module allowed teachers to conduct action research in their classes. In subsequent years a number of these teachers went on to take their Graduate Certificate or MA in English, something they would not have considered without the project making it so geographically available and so relevant to their professional concerns.

2008–10: Shakespeare Reloaded and system stress

Almost every aspect of 'Shakespeare Reloaded' caused system stresses. The academic-in-residence program was complicated to timetable at a busy school when it required staff to be pulled out of regular classes and various student classes to be combined. In addition to this recurring logistical burden, there was also the question of how compulsory academic-in-residence events were for teachers because at times the events occupied the timeslots of compulsory staff meetings and PD days. We didn't want our project to be compulsory and our ethics clearance forms mandated the easy exit from the project by any participant at any time without penalty should he or she wish to opt out. Additionally, what if a teacher is exhausted by a week of frantic busyness at the school and has just one hour to collapse with a cup of tea into mindless rest? Are they likely to, and would we want them to, give that precious hour away to some project event?

The university's Department of English felt itself in a quandary over whether teaching modules offsite at a school was inequitable to students who couldn't easily get there from other parts of Sydney. Enrolled postgraduate students were required to complete 'Child Protection' (criminal check) declaration forms because they were going to be taught on a school campus where they might encounter children. Perhaps most poignantly, as members of the project's academic team taught these modules, their teaching practices became subject to the valid scrutiny and criticism of the students who were the teachers from the PO and other schools. In the academic-in-residence program the academics often saw the teachers in their classrooms dealing with the daily challenges of teaching. Now the shoe was on the other foot as school teachers assessed our tertiary teaching styles and we realized how uncomfortable academics feel about pedagogical critique – especially from secondary level educators. This was brilliant for us because it showed up our deep-seated, even unconscious, system-ism, the very system-ism we were intellectually keen to shed.

The school paid half the enrolment fee for all its teachers who decided to undertake the postgraduate modules, but the university had trouble in figuring out how to receive a payment *en bloc* from the school. Matters became more complicated when school staff made enquiries to the university to solve their individual enrolment problems and in the process did not fully appreciate (and why would they?) the complex institutional relationships between the project ('Shakespeare Reloaded'), the university's degree program (the MA), and the department's specific module offerings.

System stress was ramifying in all directions. It was music to my ears – albeit rough music. The grinding sounds of system stress are what I live for. They mean something is happening to systems, something they don't like. Systems and internalized system habits are bending – or trying to. They never do this willingly because such bending goes against their natural logics and design economies. To cause system stress is to force a system to have an experience; ideally it would prefer to be experienceless, frictionless. To apply pressure to parts of the system by the imposition of indigestible realities from outside its rule is to force it against itself or lever it apart. This sort of buckling is the deep groan of system stress and it finds vocalisation in diverse expletives (surprise, anger, frustration, amazement, resentfulness) expelled from its human subjects whose workload and stressload increase as a result. Linkage academics can look forward to being not only scorned by colleagues for betrayal of inherited values, but also hated by the most obscurely embedded institutional administrators whose protocols are bypassed or corrupted by rogue behaviour.

Through 'Shakespeare Reloaded' linkagespace became a delicately handled crowbar in the hands of a vandal. I loved it precisely because human voices and preferences began exposing system parameters and demanding system submission. The system says you can't do it that way. It won't work. Have you thought about the ramifications? It's not equitable. It's a bad precedent. It's too hard. What you need to do is this. You *need* to do *this*. Ardenspace replies, there are more things in heaven and earth than are dreamt of in your philosophy. Here, try this. Or this. Oh, that hurts, does it? Pity.

2013: Becoming intelligible

'Shakespeare Reloaded' was experimental for all involved. We had successes and failures, but chief among the gains was our experiential learning by being system creatures in pursuit of the system edge. This knowledge, this field of research, can only be learned this way. Its paradoxes must be felt or they will not be known and the finer avenues of possibility will not be glimpsed or recognized as such because we will be out of range. 'Shakespeare Reloaded' was successful in holding us at the system edge for a prolonged period where we could begin to ask how our discipline is defined, how our system subjecthood is constituted, how creativity and imagination exist for us and our students. There's a special perplexity that comes with conducting this blend of research and meta-research, this mix of researcher and stakeholder objectives, which teases and fatigues one's professional identity. We have begun to see at the system edge. Answers, if they are to come, must start from here.

It is good to look on the truths of Literary Studies 'askance and strangely' (Sonnet 110). If we do not, we will not comprehend culture's complaint against us nor witness our own demise. We need to shrug off our naivety and become literate in our cultural position so that we can develop more sophisticated discourses of defence and engagement. Our apologies to the world are sounding tired: 'There's no mend,' our voices crackle, 'of aching books.' We cannot persist in this 'By-the-waters-of-Babylon' public voice, or not solely, because it sounds to many young people like the lingering wheeze of old men dying. We won't win respect, or much support, or a space in the future, that way. We need to be more imaginative in our self-perception and projection. We cannot always speak wistfully to the world. To do so is to demand that our students abstract themselves from their reality and abase themselves before friends and family to get us.

Despite all our protestations of our Friend's eternal summer (Sonnet 18), our relevance is slipping. If the world decreasingly comes to us in the humanities, we must increasingly go to it; otherwise, our self-love, like that of the Youth in Shakespeare's Sonnets, will be our condemnation and extinction. This is not to abandon all our truths. It is to love, not scorn, the world (Sonnets 1, 4 and 9). We need to help potential students see us in the real game, rather than see us as sugar in the coffee of more practical degrees. We need to make sure our disciplines are multiply actualized in their reality. We need to learn new skills to enable their pursuit of their desire for us in their world. We need to be more intelligible and essential to our students. We owe it to our world as its humanities deficit grows uncontrollably.

Time's 'crooked eclipses' already overshadow us in Literary Studies, and the 'scythe and crooked knife' of sovereign cutbacks are resizing our magic circle (Sonnets 60 and 100). Australia's tertiary English departments are dying off, and as diminishing bands of literature academics reconstitute into spectral 'programs' within larger schools or faculties our discipline's autonomy, relevance and contribution are bleeding out. Literary Studies is dissipating into larger Communications schools and vocationally structured systems. No-one outside is noticing, or perhaps they simply do not care, that English Literature is paling at universities and that the financial unit of the English department is in many places long gone.

As we say in Australia, it's pretty crook. It will get worse before it gets better. There's not much comfort in saying to a bunch of Philistines at that later point, 'I told you so.' By then, all they'll hear will be 'blah blah blah.' We need to care to be heard *now*. We need to practice being intelligible or Literary Studies will go the way of the Tasmanian Tiger, only studied on film.

2009: The Bard Blitz

There is life at the system edge. It does emerge – out there beyond the courts, yet in sight of them, where the exiles have their ardenspace. One pup of this forest was the 'Bard Blitz.'

Within 'Shakespeare Reloaded,' the Bard Blitz arose from the interactivity of the disparate participants, disciplines and institutional syllabi, and reified as a self-coherent, practical approach to a multivalent problem. Practical, but not entirely workable because it was not entirely practical in system terms – and did not seek to be, because the goal was ultimately to enhance learning and cause positive turbulence rather than merely satisfice the system.[5] The Bard Blitz was a learning module designed to enrich the practice of literary analysis by students studying Shakespeare's plays.

It responds to a host of secondary and tertiary stakeholder wants. English teachers in NSW want their students trained to compose the best literary-analysis essays they can: this is because it is a core skill in English and it should lift their grades in the HSC and therefore better their university admission chances. The teachers want ways to enrich their students' encounter with Shakespeare's texts to enable deep learning and creative engagement. The syllabus framework constraints of the HSC system, especially in respect to 'Standard' and 'Advanced' English, mean that students' experience in textual analysis and essay building is often limited to the evidencing of theses that have been pre-imagined by syllabus or teacher.

Across the institutional divide, academics want new students arriving at university to have been better prepared to create original theses based on well-informed close analysis of literary texts. Many conceptually interesting student essays in English at junior university level collapse because they have unconvincing evidentiary foundations in the primary text.

Students in the ultra-competitive context of HSC English want to be able to deliver essays that succeed in impressing their external examiners. Students who seek transition to university also want to be equipped appropriately so that they can build on learnt skills when they commence first-year tertiary English.

In the normal run of things: the teachers would curse the system and teach to the exam with as much pedagogical value-adding as possible; the students would curse the system and prepare as strategically as they could for the exam; and the academics would curse the teachers, the school system and the 'poor' students at every opportunity during first-year which they'd view as a necessary whitewash of the past and a new induction into English fundamentals for students. Each silo-ized category of stakeholder deals with the problem in his or her own way, without consulting the others. Each system's agents preserve their system's governing principles and dampen turbulence.

'Shakespeare Reloaded' bashed all the heads together for a while and the Bard Blitz fell out as a possible tool to help senior-high and junior-university students, and to help teachers and academics. The Bard Blitz sought to promote deep engagement with Shakespeare's texts via a four-stage, active learning task that takes close reading as its basis and original essay composition as a key outcome. The model was designed to be able to be morphed (expanded, contracted, tailored, transferred). It was built free of idiosyncratic syllabus traits, but teachers could dovetail it into institutional schemes of work and assessment paradigms. It could help students who struggle in English as much as those who excel because it was designed to motivate and equip. In the end, though, its value and workability as an intensive, guided exercise, relied on making space available in already overcrowded curricula and timetables.

The Bard Blitz worked with an amalgam of ideas from three pedagogical schemas: David A. Kolb's experiential learning cycle that charts a learner's passage through four learning modes, being concrete experience, reflective observation, abstract conceptualization and active experimentation;[6] John B. Biggs and Kevin F. Collis's 'SOLO taxonomy' that describes levels of learner understanding detectable in learning task responses ranging upwards through pre-structural, uni-structural, multi-structural, relational and extended abstract thought;[7] and Ronald Barnett's ideas of 'risk' and 'pedagogical space.'[8]

As Figure 1 illustrates, the four stages of the Bard Blitz map onto the four stages of the Kolb cycle so that close reading and essay building are united in an integrated process of experiential learning.

To begin, the students are placed into small groups of about six to eight students. The first stage is a 'concrete experience' which entails small group discussion to familiarize students with the linguistic, dramatic and story-related aspects of a single, short extract of text selected from a Shakespeare play. The teacher has preselected the extracts (each about fifteen lines in length) that are poetically rich but not too obscure so that students will, over the course of the exercise, be able to: respond relatively immediately to them; decode/translate them accurately with some effort; and, find diverse ways into relational and extended abstract thought about them and the play.

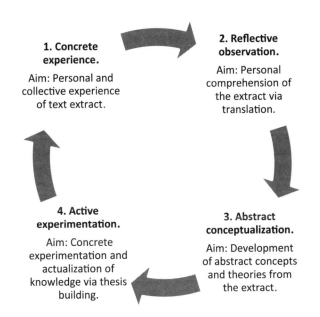

Figure 1 *The four stages of the Bard Blitz mapped onto a simplified version of Kolb's learning cycle.*[9]

Here are four extracts from *Hamlet*[10] that would work (but so would many others):

1. *Hamlet:* 'O that this too too sallied flesh...Must I remember?' (1.2.129–43; the wider text for context purposes includes 1.2.87–159);

2. *Polonius:* 'It shall do well...Your wisdom best shall think.' (3.1.175–86; the wider text for context purposes includes 3.1.161–87);

3. *Claudius:* 'O my offence is rank...To wash it white as snow?' and 'O wretched state...All may be well.' (3.3.36–46, 67–72; the wider text for context purposes includes 3.3.27–98);

4 *Gertrude:* 'There is a willow grows askant. . .To muddy death.' (4.7.164–81; the wider text for context purposes includes 4.7.125–92).

The objective of stage one is to establish a basic familiarity and connection with the extracted text so as to remove its scariness and make it intelligible. It should be a fun, diverse, even noisy, learning experience. It might include: reading aloud in various ways to foreground disparate meanings; consideration of the broader contexts of character, staging and plot through discussion and/or acting out; sharing of personal responses, including likes and dislikes in respect to the passage's words and characterization; and solving any particularly obscure bits.

The second stage is 'reflective observation' in which the students work in pairs to consolidate and demonstrate their understanding of the precise meaning of the extract via a process of translation. The point is to get them focusing as intensely as possible on deriving the exact meaning of each word, phrase and line. Unrushed attention to detail and clarity of thought and expression are crucial here. The pairs of students then share their translations with their larger group and together they all discuss the exercise and the translations. It is expected that the pros and cons of translating from early modern to modern English, and from poetic artwork to literal translation, will be directly addressed because these cut to the heart of the value, complexity and aims of Literary Studies.

The trial run of the Bard Blitz showed that the student translations are often far more general and semantically casual than the original text and there is much pedagogical space for the teacher to help students bridge the gap between the word or phrase they chose and the meanings and resonances of the original. Getting stage two right is crucial to the entire process of credible and complex thesis building, and to understanding Literary Studies *per se*, because it is all about dwelling on an artistic text in order to do justice to its aesthetic qualities and meanings. The sheer time spent here is a direct and powerful counterargument to the arbitrary, systemic exigencies of syllabus and assessment backwash.

We must be quite clear that the aim is not to turn Shakespeare into prose, nor to replace the early modern text with a modern version. The aim is learning to read: generally learning to read anything closely, but also more specifically learning to read a historical, poetic text with unfamiliar vocabulary. The students are to arrive at some detailed understanding of the early modern sentences, an understanding that goes beyond mere guesstimation of meanings which is the default move of most Literary Studies students. Translation is valuable in that it forces discrimination and precision in comprehension. It foregrounds word meanings and nuances, grammatical vagaries and alternatives, and rhetorical and stylistic aspects. It forces students to come to grips with the poetic artwork as an artwork and it combats the tendency of literature students to base arguments on general and imagined meanings that have little to do with the textual evidence. This stage of the Bard Blitz is about saying that literary study is the core business of Literary Studies.

In the third stage, 'abstract conceptualization,' the students brainstorm as a group to draw out concepts from the extract that relate to the play as a whole. Each student compiles a personal list of concepts that might relate to characterization, language use, staging, cultural context or any other area regardless of whether the ideas seem clichéd, obvious, trivial, idiosyncratic or weird. The two key points are that each student should compile a large concept hoard and each concept should arise from or appear in the extract yet relate (or be relatable) in some way to the whole play. This concept hoard will be the seedbed of their original thesis to be developed in stage four.

In the final, 'active experimentation' stage, students work individually with their concept hoard to cluster, hierarchize and/or sequence its ideas or some of them into the embryo of a thesis or line of argument that says something (anything!) about the extract and the play as a whole. This stage may require substantial guidance from the teacher, but should result in a piece of original written argument based on solid evidence and abstract thought that the student has genuinely invested in from the ground up.

In the trial run, teachers noted how difficult this stage was for students because it asked them to come up with their own line of argument rather than getting them to answer a question set by the teacher in alignment with the syllabus. In the Bard Blitz they are guided to create their own thesis that depends on close textual analysis and a personal collection and disposition of concepts. The Bard Blitz is structured, but structured to provoke independent literary scholarship of the sort valued at university. It is training in free-climbing for students who've always followed a ropes course. It gives authority to students in the practice of literary analysis, rather than dictating authority to them. It demands students become experiential learners, and teachers deploy professional, discipline-area guidance.

Two virtues of mapping the Bard Blitz onto the Kolb learning cycle are: it confirms the intrinsic relation of close reading to essay building in English and trains students therein; and, it presents literary analysis and essay writing as a complete and authentic learning experience traversing the entire Kolbian cycle. Kolb contends that his cycle's four stages are equivalent to 'four basic learning modes'[11] and that individuals develop over time an alignment with one of 'four basic forms of knowing' (or 'basic learning styles'): convergent (favouring abstract conceptualization and active experimentation), divergent (concrete experience and reflective observation), assimilative (abstract conceptualization and reflective observation), and accommodative (concrete experience and active experimentation).[12] With this in mind, the Bard Blitz gives students some opportunity to engage in the task through their natural preferences and strengths, while also helping them to understand and experience learning through the other basic learning modes. The learning experience is diversified via small group work, paired work and individual work, and blends a high degree of teacher guidance with latitude for student autonomy.

As the student is guided through the Bard Blitz he or she will be engaging in intellectual activity that exemplifies all levels of the SOLO taxonomy from the uni-structural (identify, do simple procedures) and multi-structural (enumerate, describe, list, combine) to the relational (compare, explain causes, analyze, relate, apply) and extended abstract (theorize, generalize, hypothesize, reflect).[13]

Activities located within the first two stages of the Bard Blitz tend to call for uni-structural and multi-structural thinking: determining word meanings, identifying linguistic features, describing what is being said. Activities located in the latter two stages should provoke relational and extended abstract thinking: analysing and explaining features of the text, comparing and contrasting, relating to larger contexts, deriving general ideas and hypotheses, building abstract and complex theories. The end product of the Bard Blitz, be it an essay or other form of coherent argument, should exemplify relational and extended abstract thought in order to deliver an original and exciting thesis. Yet, it will also rely on accurately conducted uni-structural and multi-structural processes in order to convince as a text-based, evidential argument. Biggs and Tang explain how each level of the SOLO taxonomy builds on the previous as knowledge increases and understanding deepens:[14] the Bard Blitz tries to take students along a similar trajectory.

If Kolb and Biggs and Tang help us address something of the 'how' and 'what' of the Bard Blitz, Barnett's ideas of 'risk' and 'pedagogical space' in *A Will to Learn* foreground the 'why.' At a time when the Cultural Studies impulse inflects so much of what we do in English and the study of language in and of itself has declined, there is a growing need to maintain the importance of training students in close analysis of sophisticated literary artworks and production of original and persuasive theses in response. The Bard Blitz is a tool to help meet this need and, in tune with Barnett's broader ideas outlined below, it is designed to motivate and equip students to conduct their own detailed explorations of daunting texts and feel confident in their own authority as creative interpreters of literature. The close attention to the meaning of the extracts also imparts important grammatical knowledge to students: this means that even those with weak vocabulary and weak grammar can read Shakespeare and learn these things from him. It affirms the need to read the early modern versions of Shakespeare and to avoid the widely available modernized 'translations' for students which steal from the student the precious experience of learning through encountering difference.

Barnett argues that the pedagogical space provided by the teacher must be 'a space in which students can make their own explorations.'[15] He uses the metaphor of the land diver – the Pacific Islander who, in an awe-inspiring precursor to bungee jumping, leaps from a purpose-built high-tower with nothing but the two vines tied to his ankles to prevent him from plunging to his death (1). More remarkable is the fact that the diver's shoulders actually need to graze the ground in order for the coming yam harvest to be blessed. Barnett writes:

> The jumper leaps into space. The leaping is only possible in space and because of space. In the leaping, there is presumably anxiety: will the connecting thongs do their work? In the leaping, there is exhilaration and there is the exploration of personal emotions. The challenge is taken on, the wind rushes, the body plummets, the ground rushes up. There is risk here, but the risk is within bounds of acceptability. ... So it is with the student in pedagogical space. She throws herself forward into she hardly knows what; but then the satisfaction comes of having tried and having emerged unscathed.[16]

Barnett is conducting a philosophical discussion of the student's learning experience in a university setting, but the analogy is valid at school too. Although it may seem extravagant to compare (as I do, not Barnett) close reading and essay building to the land diving ritual of Pentecost Island known as the N'gol, it is just this sort of analogy that is required for us to perceive afresh the anxieties and possibilities at play in the student's encounter with extraordinary texts. Close reading and thesis building remain the core business for the student of English and both activities should be, at their peak, edgy, mesmerizing and fulfilling. They should demonstrate the student's faith in the work of art as art, in him or herself as interpreter and, perhaps more implicitly, in the act of interpretation as creative and hence in some way transcendent.

At each stage of the Bard Blitz the student should be encouraged by the teacher and by the arrangement of the pedagogical space to control self-doubt and anxiety, to seize the perceived risk as exciting opportunity, and to 'leap' into possibilities of knowing and experience that would otherwise never come to be. According to Barnett, it is not the teacher's role to limit these possibilities, but to express a 'solicitude' that believes in the student's potential, and 'leaps ahead of the student, not so much as to determine precisely the journey that the student will take but to open up possibilities for him.'[17] The Bard Blitz attempts such solicitude, particularly as it enables the educators to learn (along with and just ahead of the students) the depths and riches of Shakespeare's archaic language and poetic mastery. In Literary Studies analytical precision and experiential learning are for everyone, not just the student.

After trialling the Bard Blitz we gathered feedback from students, teachers and academics. All three groups felt the exercise was valuable (at school and university) for its delivery of a personal experience of intense literary analysis and original thesis building. At the school, one student group 'appreciated the detailed focus on language. It pushes you, getting into each word, more understanding.' Another group complained that it 'needs to be more general, not too focused on word-by-word, line-by-line analysis. Felt like special-education students': yet this same group also admitted that the 'inclusion

of translation' was important in improving their understanding of *Hamlet* because of the 'focus on individual words
rather than glossing over them as you read.'

A two-hour time block would be ideal to cover the four
stages, or two one-hour segments. The whole exercise could
be done in one hour, but even if conscientiously managed, it
would create just the sort of rushed process that the Bard Blitz
eschews. Although the Bard Blitz can be expanded or
contracted to suit available infrastructures, the more time
allocated, the more it is likely to achieve its aims. Teachers
need to believe strongly in its value if it causes the reduction of
time allocated to other aspects of the curriculum. Consequently,
it is vulnerable precisely because it cannot be justified as
strongly as more tailored lessons in terms of curriculum
frameworks and protocols. Extraordinary as it may sound, in
senior-high English such an exercise is a luxury.

A teacher asked me whether the Bard Blitz and its selected
extracts could be used to help students unlock widely accepted,
significant interpretations of the entire play. These interpretations would then be part of the students' collective arsenal of
reliable interpretations that they could draw on when they sat
the HSC examination. One way to do this would be for the
teacher to gather concepts from the students' individual
concept hoards and put them all up on the board and then
weed out the rubbishy ones so that only the good remain for
the whole class to appreciate and remember. The teacher can
then be sure that all the students have 'got' the message of the
play through the isolation of the main concepts and that they
will be developing their individual theses around widely
acceptable interpretations of the play. This is good exam prep
because it will insure the students are up to speed on the basic
interpretations of *Hamlet* and not distracted by pursuing
blind alleys or idiotic interpretations that could easily be taken
for ignorance at the marking centre. The problem with this
approach is that it co-opts the Bard Blitz into the service of
convergent thinking and the transmission of authorized
knowledge, rather than allowing it to promote original and

independent, experiential learning. The Bard Blitz becomes a hoax and pointless exercise. Mr Hubert and his iron poker have reentered the room.

The system stress that this teacher's response was trying to alleviate lay in the fact that a student could excel in the Bard Blitz by developing his own interpretive authority and skills in close reading and original thesis building, and yet if he took the same approach to answering the HSC examination question he might crash and burn. He could find his unique approach to *Hamlet* penalized for being arcane or irrelevant, not adequately satisficing syllabus requirements, and thus receive the message from the educational gatekeepers that his type of Literary Studies is wrong or valueless. He would learn the hard way that gaming the system is more important than truth to the discipline or truth to oneself.

This problem is not easy to negotiate as an educator because structure and freedom must somehow co-exist in institutional learning paradigms, and teachers want to do the right thing by their students in terms of both their ideal of the discipline and the actual curriculum parameters. A recurring stress within 'Shakespeare Reloaded' was this collision of the reflex pragmatism of school teachers with the reflex problematization of academics. I believe that neither is simply correct or incorrect. They are habits learned by system creatures. Barker College, as our Partner Organization and major stakeholder, wanted the project (not solely, but significantly) to enhance their students' performance in the HSC. The academics could see that this was a logical and ethical aim given the circumstances, but at the same time wanted (not solely, but significantly) to provoke learning that broke with the system. In order to meet in the middle, which was the system edge, both sides had to be prepared to relax some deeply ingrained mental laws and to have faith that this risk might deliver new, unexpected benefits to all.

In my view, to guide the Bard Blitz to production of mainstream interpretations in stages three and four, weeding out students' quirky or flawed angles, would be rather like saying to the land diver as he is about to launch his body from the scaffold his own hands have built: 'Hey wait! Just think again before you leap because fertilizers will bless the land more effectively than your shoulders brushing the ground with just the right blend of faith and execution.' The impact of such a remark, which uses one type of truth to undo another, is profound. The student wants to explore. The educator says, forget it pal, we've already been there, here's the map. And don't forget the exam. The student replies, hey dude, where's my rapture?

It's not just ugly teaching, it's the abandonment of learning.

2013: The unquantifiable rightness of fleeing

What is proper research? Does it resemble learning?

I have learnt more, and more diversely, through my adventures in ardenspace than through many of my other projects put together. In recent times I've been researching what Thomas Herbert might have meant when he referred to ancient Persian reliefs as 'grotesco work' in the 1664 edition of his travel book and how Margaret Cavendish's books of the 1650s preserve traces of her reading of key texts by Thomas Hobbes and Descartes. These pursuits, which I love and believe in, feel like unproblematic manifestations of my professional identity as an early modern Literary Studies specialist. Yet, I seem to have learnt more fully, more metacognitively and physiologically (rather than just intellectually through a conceptual microscope) via 'Shakespeare Reloaded.' It is all about the experiential loosening up (and simultaneously, connecting up) of habits of mind. If the habits of mind of a small number of academics, teachers and students in an experimental project limited to one university English department and one school profoundly change as a result of their entering ardenspace, then when such agents move between systems they will take their unquantifiably altered nature with them.

Systems power themselves (admittedly on the flesh of their agents), but ardenspaces, like any complex process, demand an ongoing stream of fresh energy to push against steady states. While the surge persists, the ardenspace persists. As the energy fades, ardenspace reduces to a blip which soon disappears as equilibrium returns. All is system again. The weary exiles are reabsorbed into their courts where they find delicious comfort in a post-marathon massage of normal compliance and a bubbly spa of system approval.

It is always much easier not to create ardenspaces. Just thinking about it gives me a headache. Systems undoubtedly fatigue and hollow out their creatures, but exiles choose to pay a special energy levy in their decision to work against bias for the sake of critique, innovation and emergence. One thing you become attuned to at the system edge is the moment of the imposition of system. What was once effortless reflex becomes a nest of troubling choices. Yet there is an unquantifiable rightness in fleeing to ardenspace.

How, I wondered, might one achieve something similar within the university curriculum? What if you fled inwards, rather than outwards? Like Lear's dream of restorative song within the birdcage (5.3.8–19). How might you provoke emergence within a single module of study? How do you solicit tertiary leaping? It was time to find out.

PART TWO

Learning Marlowe

CHAPTER FOUR

Perceived relevance

(The state we're in)

2009: *Ladybird*

Let's set aside Linkage Projects, schools and Shakespeare and move into the realm of a single, tertiary module of study. To be exact, it is a senior-level module that I teach on that arch system antigen Christopher Marlowe. We've seen revenge effects, system stress and positive turbulence in the schooling of Shakespeare. Keeping those things in mind, it's time to explore perceived relevance and vexed liberties in the learning of Marlowe. What are the rules of play in the tertiary classroom? Why and how would you break them?

In early 2009 I went to see the play *Ladybird* by new-wave Russian playwright Vassily Sigarev. I knew nothing about it beyond some promotional material put out by the theatre. In it I read that '*Ladybird* is a savage, hilarious and haunting dissection of the futile dreams and rage of those living on the urban fringes, yearning for escape.' The play was written in 2004 and the university library had no copy of it.[1] The young playwright had won awards. The director Lee Lewis and the theatre had great reputations.

I read the teasers about the lead roles. Arkasha 'works in the blackest of black markets – he trades in stolen grave markers sold for scrap metal – and tonight at Dima's going-away party he's owed a large delivery.' Dima is joining the army tomorrow. 'No choice really – he's 19, dirt poor, his mum's dead and his dad's a drunk. The metal grave markers. . .are down to the last few.' And Lera: 'with a mother trying to sell her for sex, a rotten tooth and a rotting reputation, Lera longs for a new start in the city . . . she just needs the cash to do it.' The advertising pictures are grimy, black-and-white, doco-style shots of filthy twenty-somethings in squalid surrounds. Weeds, concrete and railway tracks.

It was 26 March 2009. I found my seat in the dark, cramped, 'Downstairs' theatre at Belvoir. It was a little square cave with tiered bench seating around three sides, the stage occupying one corner of the space. The place was full and I was nervous as hell. Actually there was no stage. It was a pile of gravel rising steeply into the corner. An old lounge, table, some chairs, fridge and TV poked out of the dirt declaring that this was also the interior of an apartment. The gravel spilled onto the feet of those in the front row and the actors, already in situ and in character, were close enough, and rough enough, to menace the audience. This was going to be unpleasant.

I had very mixed feelings because I wasn't here as a casual theatre-goer, but as an educator. I was teaching. This was my classroom. I'd told my Marlowe students that they had to see the play sometime during its run. We wouldn't go as a class; they should make their own way individually or with their friends, to have an uncompromised theatrical experience. Some of my students were probably sitting nearby. I didn't recognize any because the course had only just started. Some were probably looking at me and thinking: 'why has he made us come to see this crap?' or 'I picked Marlowe because I wanted to do Marlowe, not modern drama' or 'he even dresses like an academic when he goes out.' Worrying stuff like that.

I was nervous because the play might be utterly irrelevant to my module and I'd made my students (some probably as poor as Dima) pay good money to see it. I could feel their resentment, their scorn for me as an academic teacher. I felt I was abusing my students: the play might be full of confronting sex and violence.

And even if they were rich and it was tame, I worried that none of them would bother to see it. They'd look at the schedule of classes for the module and conclude that the Sigarev bit was patently 'off topic' and simply ignore it. Their formal learning at school and university relentlessly trained them to see only that which is 'on topic.' I feared my scheduled class on *Ladybird* in a few weeks would be a flop with a huge 'no show' of students: a resounding vote of no confidence in my curriculum.

I'm never nervous teaching, always super-prepared and relaxed.

Except now.

'In the beginning. . . .' The Waster began his narration in a thick Russian accent, and we were under way. May as well enjoy it. It's all too late now. I'd have a month to worry about it until the scheduled '*Ladybird* and Marlowe' class on 23 April.

I'd inherited the Marlowe module. It had been taught previously as a Shakespeare–Marlowe comparison, pitting Marlowe's *Jew of Malta* against Shakespeare's *Merchant of Venice*, and the latter's *Richard II* against the former's *Edward II*. When I became the sole teacher of the Marlowe module, I was keen to downplay binary comparisons, so I eliminated Shakespeare. The content became solely Marlovian. We began with the 'Elegies,' and then we went through the plays in chronological order, including 'Hero and Leander' along the way. Students would read the play that was set for each week, and some source and critical material, and we would discuss the various academic debates that had special relevance to the text in question. As an 'advanced,' senior-level module, the assessment involved just two research essays rather than the multiple and diverse assessment tasks of junior modules. The Marlowe module was popular, enjoyable to teach and undemanding. No-one in their right mind would change it.

So I changed it.

I couldn't not change it because I myself had changed through 2006–8. Teaching the Marlowe module had begun to feel like trade in grave markers. Exploitative, coercive, inevitable. Pedagogy as a parody of itself. Don't get me wrong, the module was successful by all measures. Its classes were lively, its students interested.

It was time to burn it down.

Ladybird, ladybird, fly away home,
Your house is on fire,
Your children shall burn!

The beauty of the ladybird in flight and the chance of it finding its home depend, like fertility in the Australian bush, on the trauma of fire.

2009: The relevance machine and Education

I've argued above that Literary Studies needs to become more relevant, but intelligently so, to its potential students and their world. Yet, there are types of relevance that we have way too much of at university. I'm thinking of the interdependent, systemic drivers of our research and teaching activities. These interlocking mechanisms of policy and procedure are effectively nets of relevance flung about us demanding acknowledgement and compliance. Core business of the managerialist university is the ongoing construction of myriad spheres of relevance, from the minute to the overarching, via which to enbubble the academic. The academic's professional life floats along inside glistening globes of relevance, performing scenes of fulfilment of system dreams.

Conscious compliance is matched by unconscious compliance. A failure of awareness of government agendas and university responses to them at the top level means the front-line academic tends to be unaware of how local conditions are a consequence of larger, higher paradigms. Our experience of restraints, impulses and opportunities in our daily work practices and in internal research funding streams and initiatives is often naïve because we fail to see how they fulfil relevance paradigms that are not ours locally, but do enlist us, often surreptitiously.

We might be surprised to learn how some seemingly worthy research and teaching initiatives that we thought were of local origin were actually passed down to our imagination through levels of management (with tasty funding attached) in order for the faculty and the university to fulfil inescapable or advantageous commitments made higher up. In a professional context where research money is hard to find and research outputs are demanded, academics need to ask why cash suddenly appears attached to certain open-invitation research schemes before they gleefully hop on board and feel the love. All the moral truths of our day might be there – from cross-disciplinarity to professional development to widening participation to democratization to outreach – enticing us, but before our first kiss, we could well ask ourselves how much system love we can handle. These in-house manoeuvres just as easily manipulate our research directions and beliefs as any external stakeholder pressure in a shared linkagespace.

We are deeply relevance-embedded in our system. Our system determines that which it is relevant for us to embrace and when. We should be asking relevance questions not merely of our discipline in respect to culture, but of ourselves in respect to our system. Who is determining what is relevant to my role now? What are the corporate chains of causality guiding my research or teaching? How unfree are my choices and desires and ethics?

Given the complexity of these questions and the global professionalization of Teaching and Learning, it is curious that academics in various humanities disciplines tend not to read scholarship on teaching and learning policy, theory and practice. You'd think it might be in our interest, or at least, of interest. The reason is we are way too busy as discipline-based agents of systems. Our institutions demand significant administrative engagement at multiple levels (program, department, school, faculty and higher), while also demanding research outputs and high student throughput.

We are all multidisciplinary – well, kind-of – these days. Literary critics are famous for screeching out of camp at dusk, crossing into states like History, Philosophy or Gender Studies, seizing some unsuspecting theory, often the wrong end of it, roping it to the tow bar and dragging it back to base. Then when there's a dull moment around the campfire, we stick our hand up its rear end and make it speak to our colleagues in a funny voice. Often that's just what's needed at the end of a long day. Such invigorating novelty makes us optimistic about the next day for our discipline.

So much for neighbouring states, but Education is different country altogether. You just wouldn't go there. Pack of weirdos. Ever seen *Deliverance*?

What's going on here? It is not simply a silo effect. Do we disrespect Education colleagues because we disrespect school teachers and there's guilt by association? Is it because Education is a social science and we are baffled by its 'scientific' methodologies and feel it reciprocally scorns our lack of 'rigour'? Is it because Education seems to be a discipline constructed entirely of method rather than content? Is it because the vocational bent of Education gives it a default purpose which is something we simultaneously scorn and are anxious about lacking in Literary Studies?

Oddly, many of us tend to think of Education (the vast and sprawling academic discipline) as having nothing whatsoever to do with education (what I do in my teaching in my department). Whatever happens in Education, can jolly well stay in Education. There's a sense among many humanities academics that Education scholarship has nothing to teach us. We think: I'm a good teacher already with years of experience; I know what I do and I do Literature; I don't get all that Edu-jargon and statistics in case studies. Education's just not relevant, or so we think, until our system, under the influence of the managerial rise of T&L, starts telling us it is. At that point either we'll begin to believe it is relevant and allow it to percolate our psyche, or we'll pay lip service to it to satisfice the system. We are beginning to do both.

Yet at the moment we know next to nothing about: the plethora of Education journals and books; the classic educationalists and their paradigm-making theories; newer interventions and radical research directions and debates; and the arrays of technical grammar attempting to conceptualize and explicate what occurs in our classrooms and lecture theatres. Our disregard for Education as a discipline is breathtaking. After all, we are educators, aren't we?

2009: The band of perceived relevance

Enter the tertiary classroom. Instantly, there's a further problem of relevance. It is closely related to Dr Faustus' dilemma in his opening monologue: how to think freely in a disciplinary context. In 2009 I decided to use Marlowe – who better? – to put the heat on relevance.

Good studentship is performed within what I call a 'band of perceived relevance.' This band is the zone of conceptual and behavioural relevance that the student believes he or she must remain within during membership in the module within the discipline. The band of perceived relevance is co-created, exemplified and exalted in the student's thought processes, classroom behaviour and assessable outputs. The student is partly conscious, but largely unconscious of the band and its implications for him or her. It is a key determiner of the student's tacit understanding and explicit manifestation of studentness. This understanding is tied to the student's sense of disciplinarity's importance at university. As a learner within a module within a discipline, the student is a citizen of perceived relevance. As long as the student studies at university, within each module he or she will be sent emphatic signals that disciplinarity matters and his or her band of perceived relevance will be created largely (not solely) in response to these. One of the givens of participation in a module is the sense that students, teacher and subject are all one in relevance.

The cognitive load of system change is at its maximum when the student enters first-year at university. This load declines as the student progresses to senior levels of tertiary study within the one increasingly familiar discipline and learning system. At this point, to operate within the band of perceived relevance is to go with system flows and to learn in known and relatively stress free and delimited ways. This is partly what disciplinarity amounts to, and the economical focusing of intellectual energy in this way is precisely discipline's strength and its guarantee of delivering new insights in known knowledge fields.

Yet, the student's achievement of any mature consciousness of what learning might be and his or her ability to learn about the experience of learning may depend on a strategic tearing of the fabric of perceived relevance. For me, the academic, as an educational authority in the classroom, to make public rips in the band of perceived relevance like Tamburlaine cutting his arm (2 *Tamburlaine* 3.2.110–29), is to introduce positive turbulence and system stress into my students' experiences of studentness. It is to upset the students, to push up their cognitive load once again, to provoke and even anger them. Some students will take it on eagerly and offer their arm, 'Give me a wound, father'; while others will shrink back saying, 'I know not what I should think of it' (2 *Tamburlaine*, 3.2.132, 130).

It may seem paradoxical, even hypocritical, for me to advocate above the easing of system stresses for students transitioning from school to university, and now to urge the unsettling of their tertiary habits of learning in their senior years. I see no contradiction because the contexts are different and in each case the aim is to enrich the learning experience via intelligent engagement with systems. The first-year student has just departed a highly scaffolded learning system that has foundationally shaped his or her learning habits and is now entering a very different framework: massive, accidental and obstructive system contradictions need to be addressed. By contrast, at university it is only senior English students who take the Marlowe unit: they are ideally located in terms of maturity and system experience to benefit from challenges to the way they conceptualize their learning experience.

In the first class of my Christopher Marlowe module in 2011 I explained the band of perceived relevance to my students. I then explained how I, and they, were to put the band under siege in this module. I then asked if anyone wanted their money back because this was not going to be a regular Literary Studies module. One student did. He had been bred and refined in the system and was now enrolled in this manifestation of the discipline. Here was I, an organ of that system, saying point-blank that he was not going to get what he'd come for, trained for, paid for. I was the anomaly in the system. It was looking like I'd be a problem. Other students were more positive as an early survey revealed. One wrote this: 'it is conceptually intriguing, the idea of transparently discussing learning methods and methods of instruction is fresh and I respect its honesty and courage within a tertiary environment.'

Senior tertiary students, having been institutionally shaped in a certain way, are naturally suspicious of any invitations for them to breach perceived relevance, and could well say with Marlowe's Calyphas: 'but this is dangerous to be done. / We may be slain or wounded ere we learn' (2 *Tamburlaine*, 3.2.93–4). They'd be right to fear because assessment systems and class decorum are both unforgiving enemies to protocol violators. Any academic taking this on, like anyone maintaining any ardenspace, will need to expend much energy allaying such reasonable fears of students. Students can go through a BA and even an MA without being directed explicitly to consider in any serious fashion their learning experience. At the end of a degree, many students actually do not know what learning is, or have a decidedly naïve vocabulary for and comprehension of it. As Barnett might say, we need to solicit – via intelligent, sympathetic and systemic methods – their taking of risk. We want students to feel brave enough to admit things like this following (from a survey response): 'I feel it is early first steps and important to try to break through the initial discomfort and engage with the innovation of the module.'

Academics should be intelligent originators of system stress in the cause of student learning in the face of systemic necessities. They should feel a moral imperative to function meta-cognitively and creatively in the classroom.[2] System constraints are only felt to bite when they are challenged. To expose and rupture the band of perceived relevance within a module creates paradoxes, or at least perceived paradoxes, where students are given a forced exile by and within the court. Formal courts can de-ossify and court their own potential for metamorphosis by the creation of a micro-ardenspace within modules to provoke more conscious learning.

Formal learning systems have procedural structures that distinguish right from wrong within the system and demand student and teacher compliance. Curriculum, syllabus and institutional policy constraints are the legal geography the student must submit to on pain of penalties to be paid in the currency of the formal system. These external rules are complemented by students' internal compliance processes. The band of perceived relevance is a core part of the internal processes and is vividly actualized in individual students' classroom behaviour.

Normally speaking, the band of perceived relevance is tacitly policed. To stray beyond the band is to be an instance of indecorum and cause of embarrassment in class. Beyond the band, and holding its invisible walls in place, is a surging ocean of shame. Shame, vast and tumultuous, never fully imagined, but when imagined in part, always feared, and studiously avoided. No good can come from beyond the band, only a degrading of the student's studentness (its integrity, validity and continuance). To stray beyond the band is to court disapproval by one's peers and teacher, discounting of one's value by the curriculum and its assessment measures, and worst of all, self-disappointment. To toy recklessly with the boundaries of the band or to persist in transgressing it is to take a path that leads inevitably to the undoing of studentness.

Shame patrols our classrooms, moving between desks like an enforcer, wielding more authority over our students than our supposed expertise. Shame is the big, silent brother of assessment. Assessment is the extrovert, chatty and amiable in his openness. Shame is the introvert, so quiet as to repel discussion. Assessment spells out the rules; shame doesn't need to. Together they are major shapers of student engagement in formal learning because both, when crossed, will menace.

The degree of success or failure, and compliance or non-compliance in assessment tasks is a relatively private affair between the individual student and the academic because assignments tend to be submitted, and feedback returned, individually. The band of perceived relevance and shame do have an impact here, but their primary zone of operation is the mind as it effects the student's public, verbal discourse in the classroom. Many students in a tutorial won't say a thing simply for fear of saying the wrong thing. Some won't comment even on something they feel passionate about because they feel their view does not fit the prevailing and thus approved view.

Most students – whether they will become learners who contribute often, seldom or not at all to class discussion – acquire early on in the semester a personal sense of the verbal discursive field of the module, which includes their perception of the academic's sensitivities, and they pour their studentness into this field (whether that means verbosity or silence). They plane off their own rough edges and settle into their habitus within the band of perceived relevance. Such good studentship offers many rewards: social inclusion within the classroom;

formal validation as a learner; parental, pedagogical and peer approval; and ready acquisition of skills necessary to traverse the assessment pathway to a successful university degree and whatever might lie beyond. Students may conduct excellent research within the band that expands the field's knowledge base incrementally.

In any regular class discussion in Literary Studies you (as student or teacher) probably won't talk at length about intimate details of your private life, your deepest beliefs and obsessions, your dreams, fears and aspirations, your politically incorrect or volatile opinions, or the bizarre coincidences that happened to you through the semester – unless of course these are the very topics under discussion because the text or scholarship provoke them. But even then, the intimacy with which one engages is decidedly muted so that any uttered remark is generalized before being vocalized. In such cases, a personal truth or intimate reflection is either considered too personal to verbalize or it is abstracted or sublimated into something rather different as it passes from the student's mind to the audible discourse of the classroom. Extremely left-field or entirely irrelevant remarks and observations are simply not brought forward. To do otherwise is to breach decorum, to manifest irrelevance and court shame.

Arguably, in the literary study of medieval and early modern texts, historical distance tends to make these limits even stricter. The group will readily sense threats to the band of perceived relevance and will take passive-aggressive measures (by way of perplexed or disapproving looks, a collective cold shoulder to the anomaly, and a stronger verbal emphasis on the safer fields of discussion) to re-centre the discourse safely within the band. This is because the bulk of students are system-attuned and feel acutely that they are losing valuable educational benefits for every second that a maverick peer speaks off-topic. They resent what they perceive to be a real-time draining of their learning entitlements. These are negative feedback processes via which the classroom system quells turbulence and restores equilibrium. A common, public and approved discourse, in mode and theme, occupies nearly all classroom air-time. Systems are anxious to maintain themselves. This is reason of system in action.

The band of perceived relevance often causes a personal truth to be uttered publicly as something of a lie (because it is self-censored, lightened, parodied, distorted) or it would not be uttered at all. It enters the class debate as citizen, not a stranger, and thus causes the right sort of flow or debate (rather than unexpected turbulence) in the conversation. At that point, while it may have had a relevance makeover that makes it acceptable to the ear of the class, it may kick back at the teller for its hypocrisy to personal truths. Worse, senior-level tertiary students are well conditioned to keep their affect and even (more's the horror in a Literary Studies class) their aesthetics under wraps while engaging in classroom learning. The classroom becomes a delimited, cerebral theatre of activity.

Students tend not to critique the formal parameters and expectations of the discipline as experienced within the module by bringing their experience from other disciplines to bear on the current classroom experience. They might mention the disparate expectations and processes, but will tend to swallow the disjunction between their modules from differing disciplines and submit to the band within the current lesson. They will develop a ready ability to be as they should be and think as they should think within this class here now, and then do the same quite differently for the next class. Their mental structures thus become disciplined – compartmentalized to the degree that the compartmental nature of their tertiary learning is normalized and becomes invisible to them. We are shaping them to learn in relevant ways only, to think via discrete systems that determine right and wrong approaches to thinking and habitually disregard connective and metaphoric thinking.

In class, shame is such a powerful enforcer that even the mildest brush with indecorum may be enough to ensure that a student never again breaches the borders of the band of perceived relevance. Such students (unless they are decidedly provocative) will then remain, like most students, well within the band, towards its centre, as a defensive measure. None of this means that the band of perceived relevance is necessarily evil, only that it is a powerful and limiting aspect of the reality of the classroom. Students may be genuinely engaged in academic learning within the band. However, it is a buffered zone that limits the chances of positive turbulence entering and refreshing disciplinarity, provoking emergence and educating students about their processes of learning. In sum, the band keeps learning's head down – studious, obedient, focused, oblivious.

The band of perceived relevance tells students that skeletons belong in closets, dirty laundry in the washer and dreams in your bed. A starkly idiosyncratic, affect-filled, personal observation has little value in the group discussion, and even has negative value if insistently returned to against the flow of conversation or direction set by the academic. It is fascinating that in a discipline such as Literary Studies shame should attach to the expression of idiosyncratic, intimate, aesthetic, affective and multivalent responses – unless they have been suitably disciplined and objected-up before vocalization. How on earth did embarrassment and shame achieve such hegemony in classes that at one level at least should revel in the art and ideas, fluidity and humanity of literature? One answer is the overemphasis on the conceptual, rational and thematic framing of subject content within formal learning systems from childhood onward.

You might reply to all this that a literature tutorial should not be a therapy group, nor a cacophony of disjunctive vocalizations. It should be a focused discussion to further its participants' expertise in some field. Okay, but how big is the 'field' to which we refer? How many dimensions is it allowed to have? What are the limits on the 'expertise' we are delivering to students? The band of perceived relevance is such a significantly dampening actuality that we need to consider its impact on learning and on learning about learning. I'm not talking about inducing chaos in the classroom. I'm talking about recognizing the power of equilibrium in the classroom as a system. And I'm advocating the provocation of disequilibrium. System stress in fact.

2011: Vampire Marlowe

Provocation throws stress in all directions. Consider the stress on the academic who might try to rupture the band of perceived relevance. Here's a case in point.

In class in 2011 I declared Marlowe a vampire.

Admittedly this was a long shot. But it was intended as an illustrative, pedagogical moment and I needed something that would be starkly inappropriate in order to show up vividly the band of perceived relevance. Not only that, but in the spirit of complexity theory I wanted an example that was randomly fresh and that I had not fully prepared in advance because it needed the possibility of unpredicted fruitfulness (or barrenness) when fed into the group discussion. In short, I needed to take a risk as well as confronting my students. So, in a discussion of the late-sixteenth- and early-seventeenth-century accusations against Marlowe by numerous detractors and gossips, I declared that for all the claims made – from papist to epicurean, criminal to atheist, and paedophile to chain-smoker – the one claim Marlowe's contemporaries had failed to make was that he was a vampire. And clearly he was.

There was a stunned silence.

Was I serious?

Well, I was the expert and they should believe me. But I was sounding crazy.

Some students shut down immediately; their body language said it all. They automatically refused to accept any system stress; they deflected the system stress back onto me as the academic authority in the room. I could resolve the stress, and the rising embarrassment, simply by declaring that it was just a joke and we could all move on, equilibrium restored.

This I refused to do.

I found it hard, but managed to reassert my claim more emphatically: it was obvious that Marlowe was a vampire. I had no idea where this would go or how I could make my case. In response to a feeling of emerging shame, I threw it back in the students' faces demanding they give up the evidence they knew they had from their study of Marlowe so far. I could feel that the band of perceived relevance was so strong that if I did not force the issue, it would instantly dissolve, and the class itself would force us all back on track, via some student's tactful, redirecting comment, to everyone's great relief. I was determined to refuse this pressure of the band, of shame and embarrassment, and of my fear of the unpredictable and the awkward in the classroom. I would force this experiment to the bitter end; too often in the past I'd given up in such situations.

Some courageous students took up the challenge to work with me. Marlowe does love the sight of human suffering if the plays are any measure, said one. He sheds people's blood in real-life fights, but does he bite anyone?, asked someone else. That so-called 'reckoning,' said a third, with them holding him down and putting the dagger through his skull, seems like a vampire slaying. It was halting going, but some students had decided, against the odds, to act in the spirit of besieging the band of perceived relevance and provoking emergence via verbalized circulation of the unacceptable idea. We mentioned Faustus kissing Helen of Troy and discussed what a succubus might be, and someone remembered that the narrator in 'Hero and Leander' wrote of touching Leander's naked body exactly as a vampire might with sensuous nostalgia, intimacy and a delicious urge to taste.

The whole time disapproval and shame threatened us from the stony faces of students who refused, and others showed benign perplexity at the discussion. We were in the computer room at the time. I'd brought us here to allow students to pursue the meanings of specific words that appealed to them in Marlowe via *Early English Books Online*, the *Oxford*

English Dictionary Online, Lexicons of Early Modern English, and various searchable early modern text databases. We went off to the terminals to conduct our explorations in early modern denotations and connotations. I declared I would pursue the word 'vampire.' When we returned to a single group to share the words and meanings we had found I was among those who had not much to offer. *EEBO* and the *OED* couldn't give me the English word 'vampire' before 1700 which was rather disappointing, but there are other ways to excavate the theme. In any case, maintaining my pigheaded persona I told the class I wasn't going to let that stop me and we spent a little more time discussing the vocabulary and iconography of vampires. At that point we left the currently exhausted topic and discussed other words uncovered by students.

After the class I consoled myself that my idiocy was not wasted because it had experientially illustrated how the band of perceived relevance works and constituted a valid attempt at provoking emergence in class discussion. For some students it had wasted fifteen important minutes that should have been spent learning about Marlowe. I had abrogated my authority and responsibility. I was at fault. In the twinkling eyes of some students I saw they got what I was doing and were prepared to leap after me. I felt gratitude to them, but I also saw how hard it is to believe in, to commit to practically, the breaching of the band. For other students, who never dared let on openly, a valuable seed had nonetheless been sown in their thinking. They had had an experience when they had unconsciously expected to have none – like any system experiencing the abrasions of stress. Disequilibrium was alerting the students to the possibility of other approaches to the discipline. Their experience of the expert acting as lunatic revealed how educational authority can willingly undo itself, turn itself inside out, argue for the existence of truths beyond its control. Authority can rebel, or at least model rebellion, and if not perfectly, at least it can do so sincerely. In a world where we do not know everything, and perhaps we know very little, such authenticity is ambrosia to students who want both to learn and to contribute their uniqueness to knowledge's shape.

What I was not to know during that class was that my vampire concept would come back to bite me (in just the right way) in the final week of term. More on that later.

2009–11: Leaf perpetuation and ladybird liftoff

Imagine the Christopher Marlowe module is a leafy garden shrub: the *Marlovia relevantsonia*. It has no branches, just a short, luscious stem anchored in a subsoil tuber from which waxy leaves rise and curve gradually outward. Each leaf represents the academic discourse around a specific Marlovian text. One leaf might be the discourse encompassing *Dido, Queene of Carthage*. The sap feeding its veins is a discursive mixture of knowledge and debates around boys' playing companies, early versus late work, Marlowe and Nashe, Ovid, Virgil, parody and travesty, Elizabethan politics and royal courtship, colonialism, race and gender. As the academic discourse enveloping the text accumulates year by year, the leaf grows while keeping its shape. Another leaf might be the discourse of *Edward II*: replete with sodomy, class and favouritism, the history genre and Ovidianism, the ensemble cast of characters and the semantic multivalency of the ending. Thus each leaf has its unique textual focus, but its pedagogical structure and mode of functioning are common to the whole shrub which stands for the discipline and its achievements as enacted via this module.

A ladybird alights on a leaf. She traverses the surface slowly. Green fills her field of vision. She is the student, and the cushion beneath her, with its spring and aura, is the academic discourse that envelopes her each week in class. This is what she has enrolled in. This is what learning is. This is the band of perceived relevance. The ladybird's distinct red-and-black shell makes it a little jewel, an ornament to the green leaf. The leaf wears its ladybird proudly because the student's obedient busyness within the academic discourse justifies and defends that discourse. The student will mimic it in voice and in essays and may, ultimately, in articles and books, help the leaf to grow.

> What is learning, saith my sufferings, then?[3]
> What is climbing after knowledge infinite?[4]
> What is it to teach us all to have aspiring minds?[5]

Do we academics want to create mimics who become us through repetition? To some degree (rightly) we do. Or have we other aims for pedagogy? Must pedagogy be about obedience? To some degree (rightly) it must. Is our aim to turn all the ladybirds green? To some degree . . . well, I'm not sure.

Or to make them fly?

Ladybirds can fly. They are denigrated by being associated with children who love to find them in the garden – little, inconsequential, cute pests. The ladybirds I mean. Observers often say ladybirds are inept in flight. Yet the biomechanics of the opening shell case, unfolding wings, liftoff and flight, are gently dazzling. And the clumsiness, or whatever it really is, draws our delight and empathy. Some adults fly vast distances – and surely they inhabit a world entirely other to our sense of them as decorative, inept aeronauts. Does any species call itself clumsy or ornamental? What is its own field of relevance from its own perspective?

What if we abandoned ornamental, and went for elemental? Rather than the student by his or her busy labour within the band of perceived relevance putting the seal of approval on our discourses, what about provoking the student's authentic responses within and beyond the band? How might academic discourse in the teaching of literature promote more elemental, autochthonous responses? We are back to the problem of the instrumentalization of learning: can we avoid the actualization of potentiality that destroys potential, and instead find ways to give potential back to itself?[6] This is not about causing students to abandon discipline-embedded learning, but about giving them more scope to engage with the green leaf in more diverse ways and to solicit their liftoff from it. This is to reduce the felt imperative for automatic academic mimicry by students and to provoke more expansive possibilities for their learning and their understanding of learning. It is to admit that while I as teacher may be an expert in the green plant, I do not fully own it nor predetermine it, nor should I be able to predict fully the ladybird's interactions with it. The ladybird is elemental. The ladybird is mobile. The ladybird has its views. Mobility is the ladybird's virtue and beauty – not to die in a green thought in a green shade. The plant needs to know this.

For the *Marlovia relevantsonia* to be an authentic part of a vital ecosystem, I need to allow freer interplay between it and the denizens of the cultural space of the garden and beyond. To resist this tyrannically is to demand a strict type of system engagement from students that is not only conducive to intellectual repetition rather than innovation, but also promotes 'procedural display.' According to Bloome, Puro and Theodorou, 'procedural display occurs when teachers and students are displaying to each other that they are getting the lesson done, constructing a cultural event within a cultural institution – which is not at all the same thing as substantive engagement in some academic content.'[7] It is a 'co-operative' public 'event' that fulfils the local, cultural definition of a lesson.[8]

A degree of 'procedural display' and submission to the band of perceived relevance will occur at school and university because these processes are part of the shared semiotics of formal learning. The key for the educator is to maximize the learning experience for students by getting the balance right between formalism and turbulence, disciplinarity and liberty, predictability and surprise. At university we want students to reap the benefits of disciplinary learning, but equally to be able to see the system and comprehend its ramifications. Responsible formal educational systems must combat their own default proceduralism by actively promoting metacognitive learning – and probably the earlier the better. Our gift to our students is no good if it does not call forth their unique gift to us. We should be making outrageous givers, not idle consumers. For this to happen we need to reconceptualize what is within our gift to give.

Up until 2009 I'd taught Marlowe, but I hadn't learned Marlowe. I was procedurally engaged, traipsing about the cushy leaves week by week with my students, begreened in reiteration and predictability. I was not as substantively engaged as I should have been because the band of perceived relevance enveloped me. By 2008 I realized that for all the procedural display in my classes, both knowledge of Marlowe and of what I was doing eluded me.

So we went to see Sigarev's *Ladybird*. I was anxious as I watched *Ladybird* because I was engaged. Properly engaged. I'd put away the fertilizer and leapt. For the first time, I didn't know how it would end. I could break my back. Suddenly things were at stake for me. Suddenly I watched what was going on and saw myself in action – in flawed human attempt – but at least, at last, in action. I was having an experience. I had put myself in an educational space that was not fully predetermined.

The play was brilliant and powerful – which was something of a relief because over two-thirds of the students trusted me and went to see it. The class on '*Ladybird* and Marlowe' was extraordinary. First, we explored Sigarev's play on its own terms as a theatrical event. We discussed its combination of realism and symbol, its intimate proximity of actors, characters and audience, its darkened audience space and semi-dark acting space. Having given Sigarev his due, we turned to consider theatre in Marlowe's day and how familiar or different it seemed to us as recent theatre-goers.

More than a few students confessed to this being their first experience of live theatre – and they loved it. That on its own was a major gain, but also we could not have discussed as truthfully or insightfully the early modern experience of drama if we had not been able to draw on our own personal experience of live theatre. The students' actual experience of theatre, rather than their reading and spouting of endless theories and clichés about it, enabled them to comment genuinely, authoritatively and surprisingly on the different ways audiences are engaged and provoked. They spoke about confrontation and radicalism, the effect of stage layout, and the sound of poetic language. The Marlovian playtexts and the students' diverse personal experiences of Sigarev's theatrical exploration of poverty, despair and faith among alienated Russian youth in the shadow of the Chechen Wars had enough in common, and enough utterly distinct, to invite sharp and true insights.

Relevance was expanding. It was going places we didn't expect. Engagement was transforming. It was moving beyond compliance. Learning seemed to be pointing inward as well as outward. Discovery became authentic and a gift that could be given. There was something new to be had, something new for everyone.

CHAPTER FIVE

Green light
(Altered states of play)

2009–11: The monster good

The reconfigured Marlowe module of 2009 was designed and taught to cause system stress in students. I wanted to perpetuate disciplinary learning as well as provoke the emergence of novel ideas. I did away with the two research essays of the 2008 edition of the module and reduced time spent on traditional approaches to teaching the plays and the academic discourse surrounding each. I included the live performance of *Ladybird* as a core text, and for the purposes of the assessment tasks I told students they should not read it as a playtext. Rather, they should rely on their experience of it as live theatre and in their written assessable pieces they should consider *Ladybird* as either by Marlowe or by Sigarev according to whatever suited them.

Lessons included discussion of how and what Marlowe's characters learn or teach in the plays. Was Faustus a surface, achieving or deep learner? This caused extensive debate of the play's core concerns. What about Leander? And in the class on *The Jew of Malta*, the students found the idea of the Marlovian Jew as tertiary student a fascinating analogical trail to follow. How mentally agile and adaptive, *à la* Barabas, did they feel themselves to be as tertiary learners? Where did learning or non-learning take Marlowe's characters and how easily? What motivated them to learn or to not-learn and how did the outcomes they achieved fulfil, exceed or undermine their expectations?

The students discussed the band of perceived relevance in respect to their own secondary and tertiary learning experiences. They relished the formal permission to speak about the learning systems they had endured, played or conquered. I solicited their transgression of the band and wove into most classes a blend of learning the disciplinarily embedded Marlowe and learning about their learning.

I wanted students at the end of the module to have had an authentic personal encounter with Marlowe's texts, to have had that encounter formally validated, to have explored something of the scholarly debates around Marlowe and his work, and to have gained some metacognitive experience that would influence their understanding of their learning in any module they were studying in any discipline. This may not be normal in a Literary Studies module, but it is an apt aim in a Marlowe module to seek to overreach Marlowe. Not every student agreed of course and even if most could bring themselves to agree in theory, it was quite another thing for them to agree in deed.

And then there was assessment. Frederick Reif writes: 'Educational innovations striving to attain different learning goals are unlikely to succeed if assessment methods are not correspondingly modified'.[1] This pedagogical cliché may be true, but we must now process such truths in light of the larger problem of the wholesale bureaucratization and instrumentalization of T&L. Harry Torrance is chillingly on target when he says we have abandoned 'assessment *of* learning' for the currently modish 'assessment *for* learning' paradigm, but both of these are giving way to the nightmare of '*assessment as learning*.'[2]

As educators, we should pursue curricula that are 'rich in problematics' and structures that combine 'a modest rigidity with a structured flexibility.'[3] But the replacement of learning with assessment is a real threat across the board as systems of objectives-based T&L establish their hegemonic efficiencies. It is becoming increasingly hard to hear the following truths: 'teaching does not determine learning. What students learn may have a link with what teachers teach, but the two are not necessarily identical. Through their participation in educational practices learners learn much more and much different things than that which they were supposed to learn.'[4] That human learning always precedes and exceeds teaching, especially institutionalized teaching, does not mean that the notion of teaching is meaningless, but it does mean that formal pedagogical systems must always consider how the unplanned, unintended and emergent might occur or be facilitated, hindered or allowed within educational structures.[5]

While Hussey and Smith, and Biggs and Tang exemplify how teachers can thoughtfully incorporate appreciation for the unexpected in the classroom into formal processes, educationalists influenced by complexity theory are more radical and experimental. Etienne Wenger, whose work has synergies with complexivist educationalists, affirms the uncontrollability of learning (and teaching). Institutional systems 'can easily create the impression that it is teaching that causes learning,' however 'learning and teaching are not inherently linked' (266). Learning occurs everywhere, and in formal pedagogical sites the linkage between teaching and learning is 'one not of cause and effect but of resources and negotiation' (266). Wenger adds: 'Learning is an emergent, ongoing process, which may use teaching as one of its many structuring resources. In this regard, teachers and instructional materials become resources for learning in much more complex ways than through their pedagogical intentions' (267). None of this is to assert the failure of teachers or students: rather it is to accept the incompressible complexity of learning even within formal courts predicated on the submission of humans to pedagogical systems. Students learn more, less and other than our systems require and desire of them. Systems do exert shaping force on their subjects, but they have no right to (pretend to) own the world. Ladybirds are elemental.

In the interests of disciplinary leaf perpetuation, I required students to compose a regular research essay of the type they were expecting. It would be evidentially reasoned and engage with the disciplinarily embedded Marlowe. No problems there. But, in preparation for it I required a more creative piece that would validate subjective responses and include textual analysis. These were just bits of a larger whole, a system of feedback and exchange that involved non-assessable written texts, verbal discussion, solicitation and prescription. I saw their work and they saw mine regularly throughout the semester.

I required students to keep a personal 'Marlowe journal' throughout the module in which they could record their responses to Marlowe's texts as the course proceeded. I modeled the use of the journal by bringing my own to class and writing in it during the lesson when specific exchanges or ideas struck me as particularly interesting. The journal was not an assessable product, but was crucial as a mechanism of metacognition and personal relevance-making. I required students to journal their idiosyncratic ideas about Marlowe: this granted validity to their personal responsiveness to Marlowe and provided a space where personal relevancies could be reified rather than fleetingly experienced as part of a chaotic shadow schema and then dismissed because they lay beyond the band of perceived relevance aka the dominant schema. I affirmed the importance of their subjective responses and I urged that they feed their most interesting or crazy ideas back into class discussion (as I would my own) so that we could all benefit from the most startling of the journal ideas and develop them collectively.

In response to those who say that journal keeping does not deliver 'any real pay off in academic achievement or writing development,' Martin Nystrand and Adam Gamoran[6] point to the way it promotes an authenticity of engagement between student, subject content, and the academic teacher who must respond constructively to the subjective quality of the journal. It puts the academic on the student's terms, not the other way round. It tells students that their life is within an expanded band of relevance: a notion they are not used to. Renata Phelps explores the congruence of journaling and complexivist modes of teaching and learning: 'reflective journals embrace non-linearity, enabling intermingled documentation of ideas and experiences from the past, the present and the imagined future. . . . There is no notion of "right" or "wrong" in the experiences documented by learners and variation, individualization and localized experience and knowledge are embraced.'[7] Yet, against this, is Paul Tosey's observation that 'creativity and innovation' in higher education are 'in considerable tension with pressures in practice towards efficiency, certainty and conformity.'[8]

I did not want the journals to be limited to an authentic, private, bilateral conversation between student and module and between student and academic. I wanted them to reify the shadow possibilities arising in the student as a result of the module and then to help the student speak some of those unpredicted ideas back into the public discourse of the classroom. Positive feedback loops are crucial to complex systems because they facilitate the amplification of ideas via group interactivity. This promotes system instability and the possibility of emergence. As Doll writes: 'Embracing complexity, the aim is for a process of cross-fertilization, pollination, catalysation of ideas.'[9] For me this was the most difficult challenge because it required students to ignore fears of shame and indecorum in order to verbalize publically their intimate subjectivity vis-à-vis Marlowe.

There is a simple yet powerful fear of speaking the seemingly irrelevant while one is ignorant of how it could be or become relevant. They had to learn to ignore this fear, to anticipate a positive reception to speaking ideas from beyond the band, and somehow to imagine the value of the exercise in a knowledge economy. Rather than dampening (via shame and decorum) the unexpected ideas so as to reinforce the band of perceived relevance (a negative feedback process), I wanted to encourage (via curriculum structure and solicitation) the accentuation and propagation of turbulent ideas (a positive feedback process) so as to push the discussion to the edge of chaos in the hope of enabling the emergence of new knowledge constructs.

I wrote my own one-page journal entries weekly and circulated them in class for consideration and critique so as to model the disposition to share intimate responses. In one early class in 2011 a student declared, 'Marlowe is Amy Winehouse.' The remark was so beyond the band that it took me by surprise and I think I failed at the time to deal with it appropriately. The student was emphatic and seemed to know what he meant, but the rest of us were taken aback. It gave me a taste of my own medicine: if the vampiric Marlowe knocked the students around, the Winehouse Marlowe slowed me in my tracks. I knew now from personal experience that it is not nice to be shunted into incomprehension in a public space which values displays of knowingness (and academics cherish this more desperately than students).

As I floundered, I realized that recovery from surprise and ready exploration of how the irrelevant may be relevant depends on a mind habituated to metacognition, associative thinking and creativity. Embracing complexity *in fact* is a very different thing from embracing it *in theory*: it has to be learned experientially. And it was all hard: hard to see, hard to judge, hard to suppress old and initiate new habits, hard to react rightly. Hard for student, hard for teacher. When was crap crap and when was crap pure gold? To make that call was easy within the band of perceived relevance. The call was always already made. But beyond the band, who of us could tell? It was more about faith, risk, intuition and commitment to *if*. It was faith in the judgment of the forest.

Winehouse, an English R&B singer-songwriter with a captivating, smoky contralto voice, had died at the age of 27 on 23 July 2011 – in other words, during the Marlowe module. Through the following week it dawned on me that my iPod-wired students were immersed in their favourite music at all waking hours. When they commenced the module and took up an edition of Marlowe to read, Marlowe would walk into a musical mental environment that was deeply subjective and already firmly established. His words and characters would unfurl and strut in a neural architecture already crystallized by and regularly dosed in the rhythms of loved music. When Marlowe was still only a newcomer in this world, Winehouse, a more important figure to the student, was unexpectedly found dead in her north London flat.

Gradually the idea of an artistic (though also naïve) genius and social provocateur dying at a tragically young age grew in my mind as a way of comprehending Marlowe-Winehouse. I listened to Winehouse's song 'Rehab' and found it expressed the stubbornness of Marlowe's protagonists, but overlaid this with a sense of empathy for human vulnerability. Increasingly it seemed to me that Marlowe and his protagonists including Faustus, Tamburlaine, Barabas and Edward II all refused to go to rehab – 'They tried to make me go to rehab, but I said no, no, no' – to mend their ways, to give up their vision, to fall into line.

I put this personal response of mine into my journal notes and circulated them to class. The developing idea melded with an idea brought up by another student about Marlowe's protagonists as suffering from not only isolation, but a sort of loneliness. The idea of *Doctor Faustus* as a play about loneliness had not occurred to me till now. The loneliness was not simple, but complexly imagined, as Faustus' resistance to rehab became a symptom and projection of Marlowe's own complex loneliness.

A key portal that had been opened by the morphed Marlowe module was affect. I had never realized how emotionally barren, because student subjectivity is repressed by the band, our disciplinary approach to Literary Studies had become. I hadn't realized that one valuable thing my micro-ardenspace approach was doing though its positive feedback process was inviting not just creativity into analysis, but intense and personal, emotional responses. Now if you, on reading these paragraphs, feel the Marlowe-Winehouse link is unconvincing – your experience is precisely my point. My argument is not about system-produced common ground, but about the unexpected, subjective and elemental truth of and in learning.

Every year I'm astonished by how anxious students get when required to produce assessable work that is not in the form of an essay. The creative assessment task allowed students an almost entirely open field in terms of form of response. This openness of form became a massive distraction to them because it made so much possible, unlike the simplifying and familiar limitations of the essay. Yet the student responses blew me – and the students themselves – away.

In 2009 three students wrote original plays that blended their own interests with Marlowe and characters from Sigarev's play. One student set some music by The Kinks against a recreated piece of Marlovian–Sigarevian theatre. Ever since, I've imagined the most horrific scenes in *Tamburlaine* acted to the sound of 'Some Mother's Son' – a complementarity that delivers a poignantly complex emotional experience that I find aesthetically gripping. The Kinks and Marlowe give something to each other. Some unexpected confluence emerged that was beautiful and devastating. It took me to the system edge, to an unimagined relevance, an elemental beauty: the monster good. It was a student's gift. Thank you Bronwyn O'Reilly.

I was then asked if we could get the plays performed by the university dramatic society. We did this and invited staff and students from the faculty: it was an aspect of the module that I had not planned for and it gave a deep sense of satisfaction to the students who invited their families to attend. If procedural display leads to forgetting because there is no experience, micro-ardenspaces are remembered because they cause experience. They change the students' subjectivity and habits of thought and become part of their emotional history.

And who says learning can't resemble a fun park? In 2011 my student Harry Knight submitted a creative problematization of the notion of 'ending' in respect to Marlowe's debatably incomplete poem 'Hero and Leander.' He took up the poem at the moment when Hero blushes and Leander gloats like Dis:

> With Hero bending at this point in time,
> Leander lively leapt to snare her from behind.
> And so enraged was she that without protest,
> Before the window fell to th'ensuing contest.
> The lovers laboured long and lurched about
> 'Til tragically she tumbled out.
> She fell, and fell, meanwhile Leander cried
> Aloud to Neptune – 'spare my bride!
> O lusty King, see how her lengthened fall
> Is bound for Hellespont, and death withal.'
> A pair, once joined, should ne'er long be separated.
> With this in mind, he self-defenestrated.
> His every member scattered disp'rately.
> (The softest Triton swallowed instantly.)
> There they remained, until for modesty
> The scuttling crayfish clothed 'em in sea'weeds.
> Alas the flames that nourish shall destroy;
> What wicked sting in the tail of worldly joy.
> The lesson learned is ne'er to hast'ly go
> Into virgins' temples, or commando.[10]

The entire piece of submitted work was bigger than this and included a scholarly discussion of the structure of the poem and theories of 'ending.' Importantly, Harry had footnoted his poem throughout very precisely to indicate how each word, line, metrical foot or rhetorical trope he'd used had been constructed in emulation of Marlowe's style as exemplified in his verse and discussed by early-twentieth-century critics. Now all that was good, but to be honest, the reason I liked it so much was more nebulous and more unscholarly (but the scholarly bits were my insurance!). It made me laugh and it made me catch some echo of Marlowe's impish chuckling wit in his poetic rendition of the tale. Here was serious play. Harry had found some bit of Marlowe, that vein of parodic genius that is an essential part of Marlovian aesthetics, and had recognized it as such. His evocation may not be perfect, but it wasn't bad, and his commitment to it showed that he knew that such lightness was not at all out of touch with the aims of the module.

I'll offer another example of serious play; this time with a darker tone. Kira Legaan's response in 2009 touched my heart. She began:

> Some sweat, a little fear, and a major question at hand, 'What is learning'? I realize I have never been asked anything like that before. Not by a professor, nor a teacher, and especially not of myself. And then I think 'what the hell has this to do with Marlowe? And will I look like an idiot if I don't get it right?' A few minutes later comprehension arrives. This is new, this is radical, this is a different perspective, and in Marlowe lies the conduit for all of these things: creativity, intelligence, spirituality, life. ... What questions did Marlowe want answered? What fears addressed? Are these notions really any different from the ones that drive me? What is humanity? Where is love? Why suffering and pain?[11]

None of this was cliché. It was all authentic. Her assignment delivered a reflection on her own psychological undoing or unlearning (as she called it) via the horrific experience of sexual abuse. This was pulled through an exploration of Marlowe's creative violence as expressive of his strenuous attempt to unlearn his world. Amongst the analysis she inserted original poems about her annihilation and recovery that were inexpressibly moving and masterfully written. She explored the *Tamburlaine* plays and *Doctor Faustus*, illustrated with iconic images of trauma by Bosch and Goya, and produced as profound a meditation on creativity and suffering as I have read. Here was the monster good. It emerges from beyond the band of perceived relevance. It is never known in advance. It is Faustus' rich reward.

This assessable output was faultless because it was intimately autobiographical, blending her past trauma with her present experience of Marlowe's texts which she found to be lively 'conduits' of learning and relevance. Her response was irrefutable evidence to me that we cannot know or measure all that we teach, and we should not limit our assessment measures entirely to pre-established learning outcomes. Another student had this response during semester: 'it allows me to negotiate my own relationship to being a student and what I want to achieve from my time here. I feel this unit is revitalising my own quest for knowledge.'

As Hussey and Smith write, the 'purported precision, objectivity and measurability of learning outcomes are largely mythical' and we should be cautious and discerning about how we submit to these potentially useless expressions of managerialism in higher education.[12] The truth of Hussey and Smith's monition was borne out time and again in the Marlowe module. One of the most eloquent testimonies, despite its brevity, was this note at the end of an email I received from a student long after the module had ended: 'by the way, in the philosophy essay I just handed in, I leapt.'

Ardenspace thrives, not without scars, yet beautiful, deep in the system core.

2011: Re-vamping (by de-vamping) Marlowe

Remember the vampire Marlowe? Two meanings for this turbulent concept arose towards the end of the 2011 edition of the module. First, Marlowe is indeed vampiric because the essence of the vampire is its quintessential affront to the human, its intolerable indecorum. This is what we just didn't quite get to in the class discussion. The vampire's hunger, its need to drink blood to persist, to continue to be itself, puts it ontologically at odds with the human. Marlowe executes his own form of ontological hunger as he relentlessly, in play after play and poem after poem, affronts human decorum. His plays manifest one blasphemy after another: from Faustus' 'I think hell's a fable' to the Guise's 'Religion: *O Diabole!*'; from Gaveston's 'upon whose bosom let me die' to Ferneze's ironic 'let due praise be given / Neither to fate nor fortune, but to heaven'; and from Tamburlaine's 'if any god' to the narrator's 'I could tell ye' in 'Hero and Leander.'[13]

Marlowe is the vampire who dwelt among us: same appearance, other essence. Seemingly a friend, yet savaging his human contexts and forcing us into spirals of unpleasant reflection on our governing variables and dominant schemas. Just as his so-called 'Atheist Lecture' seemingly reconstructs his listeners,[14] and his plays reimagine the possibilities of imagining, Marlowe's artistry feeds on the human in inhumane ways. He drinks and dismantles humanity. His theatre presents this horror to the audience who, as survivors of the show, must carry away its trauma inside them like a nightmare truth about themselves.

Less obviously, the vampire notion explicates Marlowe's own entrapment in a modern learning system that sucks him dry. I only discovered the following meaning of 'to vamp' in the final week of semester, but it instantly made sense. In advertising, a celebrity is often enlisted at great expense to sell a product. The cost is worth it because the celebrity gives the product credibility and market cut-through that validates it and causes widespread awareness, uptake and investment. However, sometimes a celebrity 'vamps' the product. This occurs when the product is eclipsed by the celebrity's star power and the process backfires. The celebrity is reified and accentuated and the product is consumed. The money and energy have been wasted, poured into the black hole of celebrity power from which no light escapes to illuminate the product. The mass and voracity of the celebrity black hole increase.

Our objectives-based learning systems have vamped Marlowe. Our transmission models of teaching and our unconscious devotion to the band of perceived relevance and academic mimicry make it particularly hard to catch sight of Marlowe or to enable students to do so. This is because our systems have vamped him, swallowed him, reconstituted and sold him on to students. He's been made too relevant, too decipherable, too quantifiable according to normal paradigms of teaching and learning. We've got him, greened him, but it is not him, not fully, not necessarily.

If we are to reach the indecorous genius, the vampiric Marlowe, to get a taste (not just an analysis) of *his* blood, and have it coursing through our veins, we need to find ways to release him from the vamping of procedural display, the band and single-loop learning. A micro-ardenspace can do this, but it will cost in energy and cause system stress. And in that fractured labyrinth there awaits the monster good. Ultimately the literary artists and their creative works that we study should be vamping the system, not vice versa.

2011: Persuasion to love

Vampires do not kill with a kiss, they enliven. They transform the victim (there is no going back) via a painful seduction. There is terror for the victim because the most intimate personal realities are forcibly undone by poison from beyond the band of the human. It is a persuasion to love. Anxiety first, rising to terror, and exhilaration follows. Marlowe's plays are a vampiric kiss that strong-arms the audience into new fields of imagination beyond decorum and expectation, beyond law and lore. The threat of Marlowe on stage is that he makes shadow schemas into palpable narratives. The fantasies beyond all bands of relevance are given language, duration, contiguity. His protagonists pioneer beyond the band, wrapping shame and impossibility around themselves like a cloak and recklessly storming onward. They have enormous power, in that mighty poetic line and hell-bent personal drive, to hold the dominant schema at bay, to shame shame, and drag the cowardly audience with them.

The sweeping, macroscopic armatures of Marlowe's dramatic galaxies defy normal fields of relevance and gather up a crescendo of agonic system stress. This motion is replicated internally within the plays in an infinite reduplication, not of agon, but of eros. The vampire kiss reverberates via the intimate mechanism of swirling inventories of promises and gifts that repeats a single pattern *ad infinitum* in varied scales and colours. The relentless persuasion to love of one character by another is the fractal core of Marlowe's aggressive body of work. Whether it is a passionate shepherd seducing his beloved, Jove seducing Ganymede, Tamburlaine seducing Zenocrate and Theridamas, Theridamas seducing Olympia, Callapine seducing Almeda, Ithamore seducing Bellamira, or the Evil Angel, Valdes and Cornelius seducing Faustus – an endlessly (res)urgent eros patterns human interactivity in matrices of power, desire and relevance.[15] Marlowe's vampire kiss exposes systems and governing variables by forcing his audiences into stunned complicity in transgression.

Eros troublingly oils system stress. The audience departs after the show asking: 'Where have you taken me? What have you made me think?' No wonder if such a vampire, who even dared call Queen Elizabeth by name into the hellhole of *Massacre at Paris* (24.49–105) had to be netted and impaled. Such was the system stress.

2011: *Blue Murder*

In 2011 I forced my Marlowe students to view the ultra-violent, Australian miniseries *Blue Murder* (1995). Written by screenwriter Ian David and directed in a confronting and visceral style by Michael Jenkins, this was a breathtaking piece of TV drama based on the intertwined exploits of the corrupt Sydney cop Roger ('the Dodger') Rogerson and the notorious criminal Neddy Smith.

It begins with a persuasion to love. Neddy Smith is hauled in by detectives. It is 1976. This is recruitment masquerading as interrogation. Neddy's voiceover begins: 'It didn't take long for me and the Dodger to become friends.' Neddy sits in an interrogation room, a model of tough defiance. Detective Sergeant Rogerson, wearing his trademark smirk and having rolled up his sleeves, sets to work softening Neddy up with threats, a phone book and his fists. Between beatings, Rogerson spells out the situation: 'You're out on bail on another matter Ned . . . we've got your girlfriend. . . . Attempt robbery, attempt murder, possession of an unlicensed weapon. . . . You got no aces Ned, you got no chips. You got nothing.'

In response to ongoing defiance, Rogerson takes Ned by the back of the head, cranes him backward, and puts his face right next to Ned's and speaks low and measured, relishing every word, almost kissing his prey. Both men are sweaty, breathy, tired. Rogerson says with near-erotic calm: 'Now you listen to me you cheap, disgusting piece of shit, I know your form Ned, you're a pimp and a maggot. . . . Even a low mongrel like you Ned has to learn a few tricks. From now on you're working for me.'

Rogerson leaves the room and sends in his offsider Lyle who takes a gentler approach. 'I'd like to know if you're gonna do any business with us.'

There's a long pause as Neddy tries to figure out what's going on. Fields of relevance are melting in and out of focus. He thinks the cops want money. 'I'm broke mate. I ain't got any money.'

Lyle takes his chance to clarify the objective of all this. 'Then you're going to have to work it off.'

Ned is exhausted and beginning to comprehend the shifted goalposts.

Lyle eyeballs him and prompts, 'Hmm? Hmm?'

Cut to the next scene with Neddy driving a Mercedes and acting as armed backup for an Eastern Suburbs heroin dealer that the cops want protected because they are on the take. Neddy's voiceover: 'I made a lot of contacts and a whole lot of money. In a year I was pushing more drugs than anyone in the country. And Roger was about to become a legend.'

The Marlowe students had no trouble getting the interrogation scene as a persuasion to love. This contest between Rogerson and Neddy was a mélange of power, eros and relevance. A seduction through sweaty grunts, punches and coughs: the none-too-subtle subtleties of old-style cop–crim liaison. It showed how the enduring 'friendship' of Ned and Rogerson was born of system power and erotic proximity. The scene exposed by comparison how Marlovian eros is undergirded by non-negotiable predation.

When Neddy facilitates and witnesses Rogerson's cold-blooded murder of drug dealer Warren Lanfranchi in a Sydney street, he finds himself in court under cross-examination. Neddy holds his nerve and lies under oath thereby assuring a good outcome for Rogerson who is in the law's firing line. After the hearing, Lyle says, with Rogerson looking on smugly, 'We're all very grateful. Your future's been discussed at great length . . . we've decided to give you a green light. Do you understand?'

Ned listens silently, cautiously, not really getting it.

Lyle continues. 'If you run into a blue, contact one of us straight away.[16] You can do what you like. There aren't any rules, bar one—.'

Rogerson completes the thought under his breath, '—never shoot a cop.'

Lyle continues, 'If a punter gets in the way, then that's fair game. Do you understand now?'

A silent agreement is struck, a contract, like a marriage. Before long Neddy is fully in league with the bent cops and their criminal schemes and raking in the cash.

Neddy's voiceover continues the story: 'The green light worked both ways though. Sometimes I had to do things to keep in sweet with the cops. Like the day we took Brian Alexander out to lunch and I invited him out on me boat to do a bit of fishing.' Ned and the cops tie the pleading Alexander to an old stove and toss them both overboard. He would never rat on the cops now. Throughout *Blue Murder*, the bond between supercilious Rogerson and hardnosed Neddy develops as a captivating 'friendship' within the parameters of the 'green light' contract, all undergirded by promises of gain and acts of brutality.

The positive turbulence of *Blue Murder* gave my students an authentic grip on some Marlovian realities. The in-your-face doco-style brutality of the miniseries gave students unpalatable experiences of eros in league with agon. They also saw how justice and law enforcement systems deal with their citizens and their others. The system is designed to eradicate Neddy, yet he is seduced and cultivated by a corrupt element of the system and finds himself in a contractual relationship with Roger the Dodger. The upshot is Ned's experience of 'the green light.'

The green light became a leitmotif of the 2011 Marlowe module. It stood for any deal with the devil. Doctor Faustus' contract with Lucifer via Mephistopheles gives him the green light: a promise of power, abundance and freedom to flout the rules of the enveloping system of reality. Yet, just as Neddy found that 'the green light worked both ways,' Faustus had to do certain things to keep in sweet with Lucifer, the corrupt representative of the system. Faustus, just like Neddy, was newly oriented in respect to the system and while new benefits flowed to him, certain words and concepts became newly off-limits (marriage, heaven, Christ the Saviour).

In class we discussed how the green light manifested in Marlowe's plays as characters did their deals with devil-systems and reaped the crop and the whirlwind. One of the readings on the module was Richard Halpern's article, 'Marlowe's Theater of Night,' which presented an analogous idea of Marlowe the artist making his bittersweet deal with the theatrical system in order to actualize his plays.[17] The thing about the green light is that it does not invite you into the system as a privileged native: it seduces you with intimacy and intimidation and gets you to make a flawed deal that delivers some system freedoms even as it undermines and entraps you.

It resembles the linkagespace.

The green light illustrated my solicitation of my students to transgress. Here was I, a bent academic, a corrupt representative of the system enveloping my students. Like Roger the Dodger, I caused all sorts of internal system stress and solicited students with eros and agon: with gently encouraging words and with the big stick of assessment structures to recompose abnormally their relationship with the discipline. In the Marlowe module, I forced them into a sort of contract, and they asked what good it would do them. I gave them much liberty in engaging the discipline, and yet what was the trade-off? Less time for learning the academic debates, learning the basic discipline truths, for leaf perpetuation. I had to keep convincing them that the green light was good for them, that fluttering clumsily round the room like pathetic ladybirds was somehow worthwhile. And in the end they were still the students and I was still the academic, just as Rogerson never tired of telling Neddy, you're a crook and always will be, you are on the outside and I'm on the inside, and this will never change.

At the end of the Marlowe module each time I seriously ask myself if the intensity of my recruitment of the students is not a little abusive. Why is alignment with my peculiar insanity any better than the students' regular, de facto alignment with the band of perceived relevance and the discipline as they anticipate it? What freedom had I actually given them in this micro-ardenspace? Were they just doing my creative dirty work like Neddy, enabling and affirming me as I worked the system in rogue fashion like the Dodger? Were they now caught in a liminal system-space, just as I had found myself in my macro-ardenspace of 'Shakespeare Reloaded'? If so, was that so bad?

Had I managed the green light to the students' best advantage?

Could they see better, and meta—, now? And was meta—better anyway?

If end-of-semester student feedback is any guide, the students found the turbulence I caused genuinely stressful. They said so directly. Many also said it was something they had to work hard to comprehend, but once they got it, they were grateful for its freshness. A tiny minority hated it, resented it, wanted out – probably wanted me out: that was one student's feedback out of fifty. To discuss learning as it was happening seemed revolutionary, if unsettling, for many of them. To some, the collision of Marlowe and learning seemed a little forced. To find Marlowe in ourselves was a discovery they did not expect, yet one they amply demonstrated. I discovered that if you upset the norms of formal learning even just a little, you cause real anxieties. You also get real and detailed feedback in the final evaluations. Rather than being desperate to rush out and never utter a word more, students wait because they have something to say. They've had an experience and want to comment on specifics. It is brilliant. Evaluation responses suddenly read like a knowledgeable conversation to be had rather than mere procedural display.

2011: Oh Jesus stay with me!

We are looking in the window of a suburban home. It is 1984. A domestic scene of a daddy feeding his baby daughter in her highchair. It's Mick Drury, undercover cop from the Drugs Squad who refused a bribe from Rogerson. Drury comes to the sink by the window and drinks the remains of the milk from his daughter's cereal bowl. Chris Flannery, aka 'Mr Rent-a-kill,' moves in the bushes outside and lines up his shot.

Rent-a-kill sends two bullets through the glass. They rip into Drury's gut and chest. He spins round against the kitchen wall, his body throwing blood from the wounds. Some of my Marlowe students cover their eyes. The baby, from the imprisonment of its highchair, screams for mummy. Drury staggers out into the living room where his wife sits with their other small child, 'Pam, help! Help me, I think I've been shot.'

What follows has been described by reviewers as one of the most harrowing and realistic representations of a man dying. Pam, cradling her child, dials emergency. Drury, unsteady on his feet, takes the phone, tells Pam to hide the kids.

'Signal One. I'm a policeman. I've been shot. 4124 Neridah St.—.' Blood soaks through his fingers and over his belt and jeans. He collapses to the carpet.

'Oh Jesus. Oh Jesus stay with me.' Drury's voice is desperate, yet muffled, speaking into the carpet, sobbing. 'Oh Jesus stay with me, please God.' He's trying to lift his head, his body surging and grunting in trauma. 'Oh, Jesus—.'

Pam, calling from out of shot, 'Michael! I'm coming.'

'Jesus I don't want to die like this. Where are the kids?'

'The kids are okay baby. They're okay. You're gonna be fine. It's gonna be alright.' He's prone in his blood on the carpet. His guts in shreds.

'Oh Jesus stay with me please Lord.' Weaker now. 'I don't want to die like this.' Faintly. 'I just want to hold my kids.' Fading. 'Please.'

This was the opening of the 'Black Angus' episode of *Blue Murder*. It leaves viewers – and my students – silent, wrenched.

Wrenched, but ready. Ready to receive another man facing death. In his own words:

The devil will come, and Faustus must be damned.
O, I'll leap up to my God! Who pulls me down?
See, see where Christ's blood streams in the firmament!
One drop would save my soul, half a drop. Ah, my Christ!
Ah, rend not my heart for naming of my Christ!
Yet will I call on him. O, spare me, Lucifer!
Where is it now? 'Tis gone; and see where God
Stretcheth out his arm and bends his ireful brows!
Mountains and hills, come, come and fall on me,

And hide me from the heavy wrath of God!
No, no!
. . .
My God, my God, look not so fierce on me!
    Enter [Lucifer, Mephistopheles, and other] devils.
Adders and serpents, let me breathe a while!
Ugly hell, gape not. Come not, Lucifer!
I'll burn my books. Ah, Mephistopheles!
[The Devils] exeunt with him.

(*Faustus*, 14.73–83, 117–20)

Blue Murder gave us back the Faustian agony of dying badly. The real, indecorous, desperate agony. Too often the final speech of *Doctor Faustus* is subjected to purely rhetorical analysis in counterpoint to his opening speech. But what if the personal terror of Faustus' death is restored? The sweat and spit of emotional distress, the physiological intimacy, the desperation of belief and confusion and terror, like Drury bleeding out.[18]

What if the opening speech of *Doctor Faustus* where he addresses the disciplines with such academic cleverness is irreconcilably complemented by his supernatural murder scene which amounts to an emotional evisceration that leaves him exhausted and destroyed? Similarly, the Drury episodes of *Blue Murder* began with Drury's voiceover explaining the cool, analytical thrill he gets from undercover work. He spoke as one in total, voluntary control of the system, as if his supreme intelligence and moral right put him well in advance of his stupid, criminal associates whom he worked to undo. Not only did Drury's mastery and mockery parallel Faustus', but his undercover operations pulled Marlowe's own potential Elizabethan spywork and death into relevance. All of this bundled together in a complex web of fact and fiction, system and subjectivity, mind and affect, early modernity and modernity.

In 2011 I invited Ian David, the writer of *Blue Murder*, to co-teach the Marlowe module with me. He brought to it a creative writer's eye for good storytelling. More than that, he knew, like Marlowe, what it meant to address risky themes in fictional work. He shared with students how he used to meet with the real Michael Drury who in the miniseries and in real life had survived Rogerson's attempt on his life. He explained to the students how dealing with bent cops and incarcerated criminals brought authenticity and power to stories, but also dangers. Ian received death threats. The premiere of *Blue Murder* was delayed by years due to an appeal by the imprisoned Neddy Smith in the early 1990s. Ian's home was broken into and ransacked, his computers and creative works taken, probably by police who feared he knew more than he did of corrupt dealings. You could hear a pin drop in the Marlowe class.

Then one plucky student asked Ian, 'Did it give you a buzz?' My jaw dropped.

Ian said, with his characteristic gentleness, 'What?'

'Did it give you a buzz that you were burgled while writing *Blue Murder*? Did it excite you, drive you harder?'

There was a pause.

'No, I had a breakdown. Couldn't write for two years.'

Silence poured through the class like a torrent.

Bloody heck, I thought, now we are learning. A powerful glimpse of Marlowe seemed to be shimmering into view – like never before. Out there at the system edge where known reality fails, we were having a reality check. Somehow, by heading away from him, we had stumbled upon realizations of Marlowe that shook us.

Ian ran the class on *Massacre at Paris*, with me assisting. He gave a screenwriter's – not an academic's – take on the corrupted text as we have it. The micro-ardenspace of the Marlowe module flourished as a complex system. Ian was a writer of dangerous fiction for big TV audiences and Marlowe a writer of dangerous political theatre for the masses. The extreme lives of Rogerson, Neddy and Drury took Ian into worlds on the edge of chaos where systems of mateship and violence turned themselves inside out and left no-one unchanged. Bent cop, exalted crook, mis-stepping undercover agent and creative artist, their fields of relevance bleeding traumatically, yet ecstatically, into one another. The artwork emerging, never easily, magnificently. There was Marlowe amongst it all, in a terrible weave of Elizabethan crime, commerce and covert ops that fuelled his creative responsivity. Overconfident and over-fragile, he sparkled in a sky of system possibility and outrage. For just a moment, a stress pattern flared signaling a life experienced. His art his gift. My students too were there, noble, resilient, generous – ladybird system creatures with much to give. More than they knew. And the module said 'give.' We were beyond 'slender trifles' and 'freshman's suppositions' (*Faustus*, 7.49, 56), beyond procedural display and the band of perceived relevance. Among the monsters good. Right where we needed to be.

EPILOGUE

Formal pedagogy is an efficiency landscape. It is increasingly dominated at secondary and tertiary levels by reason of system. Teaching and learning are being reified in particular ways that produce unassailable system goods characterized by predetermination, pro forma-language, quantification and instrumentalization. Revenge effects including backwash, mimicry, proceduralism, reiteration and surface learning, as well as perceived relevance, canalization, single-loop thinking and ignorance about learning, abound. I began this book with Shakespeare's Hubert and Marlowe's Faustus as teacher and academic caught in educational systems that impose constraints on knowing and knowledge. Their humanity and imagination were the keys that unlocked the strictures of formal courts of learning to enable the liberating potentiality of exile. Once they are released into a world of choice and contingency we cannot ignore the fact that the freed student Arthur dies by his own misjudgment (*John*, 4.3.1–10) and the rebel teacher Faustus pitches himself into eternal confusion (*Faustus*, 14.62–120). The stark and secure clarity of courtly life is replaced by perilous half-light at the system edge. It is easy to trip or lose one's way in pursuit of emergence and the monster good – yet to not risk the former, is to not find the latter.

There is no entirely fresh start for system creatures and no easy road for exiles. Our language is always tainted by machine language. Despite the perils, there is an unquantifiable rightness in flight because it is the best way to become educated about education. Our voices can be our own, but we need to reduce system noise to hear them. The forest is our best chance to hear what we need to hear, to get traction on the seemingly intractable. Our students, our literary artists, ourselves, deserve no less.

'Shakespeare Reloaded' came to its conclusion at the end of 2010. We applied for a larger, internationally networked Linkage Grant to continue our work from 2011, but were unsuccessful. Our collaboration with Barker College seemed set to end. But I'd been blooded by the first project and so, like Faustus, readily drew up a second contract. This time I didn't go through the Australian Research Council, but went direct to Barker College. We successfully negotiated a new, co-funded project called, 'Better Strangers: Complexity and Creativity in English and Drama Teaching' (2011–13). Without realizing it I had moved to the next stage of entrepreneurialism, the category of externally funded research agreement initiated by the academic and outside the regular ARC system.

I realize full well that the 'Shakespeare Reloaded' project and its sequel are not intensely radical and complicated commercial humanities arrangements, but the point is that they have changed *me* as a researcher, given me market skills, knowledge and confidence, as well as an eye to future market possibilities. I'm different now – and more paradoxical. My view of academic research and teaching has been put into an expandatron (as my six-year-old says) and there's no shrinkatron around for unthinking my new thoughts.

The creation of ardenspaces continues to compel me because I cannot now un-see systems and I believe important things are visible only from exile spaces. Where all this will lead is anybody's guess, but it is imperative that we use our humanity and imagination to rediscover potential in learning – outside, inside and between systems.

I'll end with an anecdote which, like the wallaby incident, really occurred. It made me feel I was being enveloped in a metaphor that critiqued the direction my professional life had taken. In 2010, after signing the 'Better Strangers' contract with Barker College, I ran back to Hornsby train station feeling very proud of myself as an academic entrepreneur. I came up the stairs and saw the train waiting at the platform, doors open. I launched inside, the doors shut and I took a well-earned seat for my ride back to university.

The train pulled away slowly . . . and into a siding where it parked.

I looked about. The train was empty except for me. The doors wouldn't open and there was no platform.

I ran through the carriages seeking help. At last I glimpsed the driver walking off outside. I banged on the glass as hard as an academic can. He saw me, looked startled, returned to the train, and opened the door.

'Were you asleep?!' he bellowed.

I was astonished. No, I wasn't asleep. I was extremely awake. I'd done nothing wrong except hop on a train just before it pulled out, rather efficiently I thought.

I found out later that the train had terminated at the station and all the people had been instructed to alight just seconds before I came up the stairs and leapt on. Bristling with pride, I'd swaggered onto a train to nowhere.

Somewhere deep in the Sydney bush I was sure I could hear a wallaby laughing.

NOTES

Prologue

1 I cite A.R. Braunmuller's edition of *King John*.
2 Throughout this book I use the Romany and Lindsey edition of Marlowe's plays and Orgel's edition for the poems. Faustus' monologue is scene 1, lines 1–66.
3 For a powerful statement of the coercive logics of formal education with which this book has some affinities, see Bourdieu and Passeron's 'Foundations of a Theory of Symbolic Violence,' in Bourdieu and Passeron, 1–68.

Chapter one: Revenge effects

1 I use the Katherine Duncan-Jones's Arden edition of *Shakespeare's Sonnets*.
2 See the 'Linkage Projects' page on the ARC website.
3 On revenge effects, see E. Tenner, *Why Things Bite Back*.
4 In this and following paragraphs I refer the websites of MySchool, MyUniversity, NAPLAN, NAP, ACARA, TEQSA, AQF and 'Mission-Based Compacts.' See bibliography for details.
5 Nicole Mockler, 'Reporting the "Education Revolution".' See also Thompson and Cook, 'Manipulating the Data.'
6 Thompson and Cook, 'Manipulating the Data.'
7 Brawley et al., 'Learning Outcomes Assessment and History.'
8 Raewyn Connell, 'Good Teachers on Dangerous Ground,' p. 200
9 Ibid., p. 218, italics in original.
10 In this paragraph I quote from and refer to Lewis, 'Rethinking,' pp. 587–95; see also his, 'Architecture of Potentiality' and the references to Agamben in both essays.
11 On the relationship between quality teaching and quality assurance regimes, see: Filippakou and Tapper, 'The State and the

Quality Agenda' and 'Quality Assurance in Higher Education'; and Collini, *What Are Universities for?*, pp. 106–11. On NAPLAN's revenge effects on children and teachers, see Topsfield, 'NAPLAN: Is it worth it?'; Thompson and Cook, 'Manipulating the Data.'

12 See Board of Studies (NSW), 'The Numbers,' in the *2012 HSC Media Guide*.

13 For example, Michael Carr-Gregg, *Surviving Year 12: A Sanity Kit for Students and their Parents*.

14 Elton, *Teaching in Higher Education: Appraisal and Training*, p. 92.

15 Biggs and Tang, *Teaching for Quality Learning at University*, p. 197.

16 Jagger on S. Smith (reporter), 'HSC Pressures Drive Students to Plagiarise,' *Lateline* TV report. Australian Broadcasting Corporation, broadcast on 11 November 2011.

17 Ibid.

18 On surface, deep and achieving learning see: Biggs and Tang, *Teaching for Quality Learning at University*, pp. 24–31, 90–1; Chalmers and Fuller, *Teaching for Learning at University*, pp. 6–8.

19 Reported in Stevenson, 'Coaching Culture Needs to End, Say Top HSC Students.' Quotations in the rest of this paragraph derive from this article.

20 Atherton, 'Public intellectuals and the Schoolteacher Audience,' pp. 93–4.

21 Board of Studies, 'Years 7–10 Syllabus Course Descriptions,' p. 12.

22 Ibid., p. 11.

23 The information below derives primarily from Board of Studies, 'English Stage 6 Prescriptions. . .2009–2012.'

24 Board of Studies, 'English Stage 6 Prescriptions . . . 2006–2008,' pp. 10, 17.

Chapter two: Positive turbulence

1 See Torrance 'Assessment *as* Learning?'; Sadler, 'Perils'; and Jessop, McNab and Gubby, 'Mind the Gap'.

2 Gryskiewicz, *Positive Turbulence: Developing Climates for Creativity, Innovation and Renewal*.

3 I refer to Dusinberre's edition of *As You Like It*, 2.1.23.

4 Biggs and Tang, *Teaching for Quality Learning at University*, p. 41.

5 See: Argyris and Schön, *Theory in Practice*, pp. 18–19; Argyris, *Reasoning, Learning and Action*, pp. 88, 104–6; and Argyris, *Organizational Learning*, pp. 67–71.

6 Argyris, *Organizational Learning*, p. 68.

7 Argyris and Schön, *Theory in Practice*, p. 19

8 Ibid.; Argyris, *Organizational Learning*, p. 69.

9 See Tosey, 'Interfering with the Interference.'

10 See Argyris and Schön, *Theory in Practice*, pp. 68–9, 87; Argyris, *Reasoning, Learning, and Action*, pp. 87, 102; and Argyris, *Organizational Learning*, pp. 180, 182.

11 Argyris and Schön, *Theory in Practice*, pp. 86–92

12 Stacey, *Complexity and Creativity in Organizations*, pp. 23–45, 72–117.

13 Stacey, Griffin and Shaw, *Complexity and Management: Fad or Radical Challenge to Systems Thinking?*, pp. 186–93.

14 Stacey, *Managing the Unknowable*, pp. 43–79; Stacey, *Complexity and Creativity in Organizations*, pp. 72–106; and Stacey, Griffin and Shaw, *Complexity and Management*, pp. 146–50.

15 Stacey, *Complexity and Creativity in Organizations*, pp. 84–5.

16 Ibid., pp. 107–240.

17 Ibid., pp. 62–3, 264–5.

18 Garber, 'The Education of Orlando,' in Braunmuller and Bulman (eds.), *Comedy from Shakespeare to Sheridan*.

19 Kuhn, 'Much Virtue in *If*.'

20 *As You Like It*, 5.4.123–48; Traub, *Desire and Anxiety*, p. 128.

21 Stacey, *Managing the Unknowable*, pp. 53–4.

22 Traub, *Desire and Anxiety: Circulations of Sexuality in Shakespearean Drama*, pp. 128–9.

23 Ibid., p. 129.

Chapter three: Shakespeare Reloaded

1 Lewis, 'Rethinking the Learning Society,' pp. 592–8.

2 See also Colnan and Semler, 'Shakespeare Reloaded (2008–10).'

3 Our project also fitted with Barker College's strategic plan, brand, and commitment to the 'Teaching for Understanding' (TfU) pedagogical model. On TfU, see Perkins, *Smart Schools*.

4 For the book arising from the conference, see Flaherty, Gay and Semler, *Teaching Shakespeare beyond the Centre*.

5 For more detail see Semler, 'The Shakespeare Reloaded Bard Blitz.' The Bard Blitz was trialled in two Year 12 Advanced English classes toward the end of their study of *Hamlet* at Barker College on 10 June 2009. My thanks to the two English teachers, Bradley Moar and Steven Allan, who co-ran the exercise with me and Linzy Brady. Carolyn Wright, Head of English at Robert Townson High School in Raby, Sydney, successfully trialled a morphed version of it with Year 10 students studying *Othello* in 2011. The Bard Blitz benefitted from input from my colleagues Penny Gay, Kate Flaherty, Linzy Brady, Brigid Rooney and Jan Shaw.

6 Kolb, *Experiential Learning*, pp. 40–2.

7 Biggs and Collis, *Evaluating the Quality of Learning*, pp. 23–8. See also Biggs and Tang, *Teaching for Quality Learning at University*, pp. 87–90.

8 Barnett, *A Will to Learn*, pp. 139–50.

9 Based on Figure 3.1 from Kolb, *Experiential Learning*, p. 42.

10 I refer to *Hamlet* (Second Quarto) edited by Thompson and Taylor.

11 Kolb, *Experiential Learning*, pp. 68–9.

12 Ibid., pp. 76–8.

13 Biggs and Tang, *Teaching for Quality Learning at University*, pp. 88–91.

14 Ibid., p. 90.

15 Barnett, *A Will to Learn*, p. 142.

16 Ibid., reproduced with the kind permission of Open University Press. All rights reserved.

17 Ibid., p. 130.

Chapter four: Perceived relevance

1 I ordered one; see Sigarev, *Ladybird*.

2 On metacognition and education, see: Tarricone, *The Taxonomy of Metacognition*; and Hacker, Dunlosky and Graesser, *Handbook of Metacognition in Education*.

3 *1 Tamburlaine*, 5.1.160, modified.

4 *1 Tamburlaine*, 2.6.64, modified.

5   *1 Tamburlaine*, 2.6.60, modified.
6   Lewis, 'Rethinking the Learning Society,' p. 588.
7   Bloome, Puro and Theodorou, 'Procedural Display and
    Classroom Lessons,' p. 272. See also, Nystrand and Gamoran,
    'Instructional Discourse, Student Engagement, and Literature
    Achievement.'
8   Ibid., p 266.

Chapter five: Green light

1   Reif, *Applying Cognitive Science to Education*, p. 398.
2   Torrance, 'Assessment *as* Learning?', p. 282.
3   Doll, 'Complexity and the Culture of Curriculum,'
    p. 202.
4   Osberg, Biesta and Cilliers, 'From Representation to Emergence,'
    p. 207.
5   Hussey and Smith, 'The Trouble with Learning Outcomes'; Biggs
    and Tang, *Teaching for Quality Learning at University*,
    pp. 99–100, 125, 171, 215–16; and Dalke et al., 'Emergent
    Pedagogy.'
6   Nystrand and Gamoran, 'Instructional Discourse, Student
    Engagement, and Literature Achievement,' p. 268.
7   Phelps, 'The Potential of Reflective Journals in Studying
    Complexity "In Action",' pp. 39–40.
8   Tosey, 'Interfering with the Interference,' p. 30.
9   Doll, 'Complexity and the Culture of Curriculum,' p. 202.
10 My thanks to Harry for creating this and letting me use it.
11 My thanks to Kira for letting me use her amazing work.
12 Hussey and Smith, 'The Trouble with Learning Outcomes,'
    p. 229.
13 *Faustus*, 5.129; *Massacre*, 2.66; *Edward II*, 1.14; *Jew*, 5.5.123; *2
    Tamburlaine*, 5.1.200; and 'Hero and Leander,' 1.65.
14 Kuriyama, *Christopher Marlowe: A Renaissance Life*,
    pp. 126–34.
15 See: Marlowe, 'The Passionate Shepherd to his Love' (*Complete
    Poems*, p. 207); *Dido*, 1.1.23–49; *1 Tamburlaine*, 1.2.82–105,
    165–211; *2 Tamburlaine*, 4.2.37–57; *2 Tamburlaine*, 1.2.19–53;
    Jew, 4.2.91–101; and *Faustus*, 1.76–154.

16 In Australasian slang a 'blue' is 'an argument; a fight or brawl' (*OED Online*, *s.v.* 'blue, *n.*', 17b).

17 Halpern, 'Marlowe's Theater of Night.'

18 Unlike Faustus, Drury survives. But the audience and Drury himself think he will die.

BIBLIOGRAPHY

Argyris, Chris. *On Organizational Learning*. 1992; 2nd edn, 1999; rpt. Oxford: Blackwell, 2008.

—— *Reasoning, Learning, and Action: Individual and Organizational*. San Francisco: Jossey-Bass, 1982.

—— and Donald A. Schön. *Theory in Practice: Increasing Professional Effectiveness*. San Francisco: Jossey-Bass, 1974.

Ashby, W. R. *Design for a Brain*. New York: Wiley, 1952.

Atherton, Carol. 'Public Intellectuals and the Schoolteacher Audience: The First Ten Years of the *Critical Quarterly*,' *English* 58 (2009): 75–94.

Australian Curriculum, Assessment and Reporting Authority (ACARA). <http://www.acara.edu.au/default.asp> Accessed 17 January 2013.

Australian Qualifications Framework (AQF). <http://www.aqf.edu.au/> Accessed 17 January 2013.

Australian Research Council (ARC). <http://www.arc.gov.au/default.htm> Accessed 17 January 2013.

Barnett, Ronald. *A Will to Learn: Being a Student in an Age of Uncertainty*. New York: Open University Press, 2007.

Biggs, John B., and Kevin F. Collis. *Evaluating the Quality of Learning: The SOLO Taxonomy (Structure of the Observed Learning Outcome)*. New York: Academic Press, 1982.

Biggs, John, and Catherine Tang. *Teaching for Quality Learning at University: What the Student Does*. 4th edn, 1999; rev. Maidenhead: Open University Press, 2011.

Bloome, David, Pamela Puro, and Erine Theodorou. 'Procedural Display and Classroom Lessons,' *Curriculum Inquiry* 19.3 (1989): 265–91.

Board of Studies (New South Wales). '2006 Notes from the Marking Centre, English Standard/Advanced.' Sydney: Board of Studies, 2007.

—— '2007 Notes from the Marking Centre, English Standard and Advanced.' Sydney: Board of Studies, 2008.

—— *2012 HSC Media Guide*. <http://www.boardofstudies.nsw.
edu.au/news-media/media-guide-2012/index.html> Accessed
17 January 2013.

—— 'English Stage 6 Prescriptions: Area of Study, Electives and
Texts, Higher School Certificate 2006–2008.' Sydney: Board of
Studies, Updated September 2006.

—— 'English Stage 6 Prescriptions: Area of Study, Electives and
Texts, Higher School Certificate 2009–2012.' Sydney: Board of
Studies, Updated March 2008.

—— 'HSC English (Advanced) Course Module B: Critical Study
of Texts. Support Document.' Sydney: Board of Studies, 4
September 2007.

—— 'Years 7–10 Syllabus Course Descriptions.' Sydney: Board of
Studies, February 2007.

Bourdieu, Pierre, and Jean-Claude Passeron. *Reproduction in
Education, Society and Culture*. Trans. Richard Nice. 2nd edn,
1990; rpt. London: SAGE, 2013.

Brawley, Sean, Jennifer Clark, Chris Dixon, Lisa Ford, Shawn Ross,
Stuart Upton, and Erik Nielson. 'Learning Outcomes Assessment
and History: TEQSA, the After Standards Project and the QA/QI
Challenge in Australia,' *Arts and Humanities in Higher
Education* 12.1 (2012): 20–35.

Carr-Gregg, Michael. *Surviving Year 12: A Sanity Kit for Students
and their Parents*. Sydney: Finch Publishing, 2004.

Chalmers, Denise, and Richard Fuller. *Teaching for Learning at
University*. London and New York: Routledge Falmer, 1996.

Collini, Stefan. *What Are Universities For?* London: Penguin,
2012.

Colnan, Shauna, and L. E. Semler. 'Shakespeare Reloaded (2008–10):
A School and University Literature Research Collaboration,'
Australian Literary Studies for Schools 1 (2009). <http://www.
australianliterarystudies.com.au/alsforschools.html> Accessed
24 May 2013.

Connell, Raewyn. 'Good Teachers on Dangerous Ground: Towards a
New View of Teacher Quality and Professionalism,' *Critical
Studies in Education* 50.3 (2009): 213–29.

Dalke, Anne French, Kim Cassidy, Paul Grobstein, and Doug Blank.
'Emergent Pedagogy: Learning to Enjoy the Uncontrollable—And
Make it Productive,' *Journal of Educational Change* 8 (2007):
111–30.

David, Ian (screenplay), and Michael Jenkins (dir.). *Blue Murder*. Australian Film Finance Corporation, Southern Star Entertainment and Australian Broadcasting Corporation, 1995.

Doll, William E. 'Complexity and the Culture of Curriculum,' *Educational Philosophy and Theory* 40.1 (2008): 190–212.

Elton, Lewis. *Teaching in Higher Education: Appraisal and Training*. London: Kogan Page, 1987.

Filippakou, Ourania, and Ted Tapper. 'Quality Assurance in Higher Education: Thinking beyond the English Experience,' *Higher Education Policy* 20 (2007): 339–60.

———— 'The State and the Quality Agenda: A Theoretical Approach,' *Higher Education Policy* 23 (2010): 475–91.

Flaherty, Kate, Penny Gay and L. E. Semler (eds). *Teaching Shakespeare beyond the Centre: Australasian Perspectives*. Houndmills: Palgrave Macmillan, 2013.

Garber, Marjorie. 'The Education of Orlando,' in A. R. Braunmuller and J. C. Bulman (eds), *Comedy from Shakespeare to Sheridan: Change and Continuity in the English and European Dramatic Tradition. Essays in Honor of Eugene M. Waith*. Newark: University of Delaware Press, 1986. Pp. 102–12.

Gryskiewicz, Stanley S. *Positive Turbulence: Developing Climates for Creativity, Innovation and Renewal*. San Francisco: Jossey-Bass, 1999.

Hacker, Douglas J., John Dunlosky, and Arthur C. Graesser (eds). *Handbook of Metacognition in Education*. New York and London: Routledge, 2009.

Halpern, Richard. 'Marlowe's Theater of Night: *Doctor Faustus* and Capital,' *ELH* 71 (2004): 455–95.

Hussey, Trevor, and Patrick Smith. 'The Trouble with Learning Outcomes,' *Active Learning in Higher Education* 3.3 (2002): 220–33.

Jessop, Tansy, Nicole McNab, and Laura Gubby. 'Mind the Gap: An Analysis of How Quality Assurance Processes Influence Programme Assessment Patterns,' *Active Learning in Higher Education* 13.2 (2012): 143–54.

Kolb, David A. *Experiential Learning: Experience as the Source of Learning and Development*. New Jersey: Prentice Hall, 1984.

Kuhn, Maura Slattery. 'Much Virtue in *If*,' *Shakespeare Quarterly* 28 (1977): 40–50.

Kuriyama, Constance Brown. *Christopher Marlowe: A Renaissance Life*. Ithaca and London: Cornell University Press, 2002.

Lewis, Tyson E. 'Rethinking the Learning Society: Giorgio Agamben on Studying, Stupidity, and Impotence,' *Studies in Philosophical Education* 30 (2011): 585–99.

———— 'The Architecture of Potentiality: Weak Utopianism and Educational Space in the Work of Giorgio Agamben,' *Utopian Studies* 23.2 (2012): 355–73.

Macdonald, Emma. 'Fears over Stressed Children as How-to Books Race off the Shelves,' *The Sydney Morning Herald*. 18 March 2013.

Marlowe, Christopher. *The Complete Plays*. Ed. by Frank Romany and Robert Lindsey. London: Penguin, 2003.

———— *The Complete Poems and Translations*. Ed. by Stephen Orgel. 1971; rev. London: Penguin, 2007.

Mission-Based Compacts. <http://www.innovation.gov.au/Research/Missionbasedcompacts/pages/default.aspx> Accessed 17 January 2013.

Mockler, Nicole. 'Reporting the "Education Revolution": myschool. edu.au in the Print Media,' *Discourse: Studies in the Cultural Politics of Education* 34.1 (2013): 1–16.

My School. <http://www.myschool.edu.au/> Accessed 17 January 2013.

My University. <http://myuniversity.gov.au/> Accessed 17 January 2013.

National Assessment Program (NAP). <http://www.nap.edu.au/> Accessed 17 January 2013.

National Assessment Program: Literacy and Numeracy (NAPLAN). <http://naplan.edu.au/> Accessed 17 January 2013.

Nystrand, Martin, and Adam Gamoran. 'Instructional Discourse, Student Engagement, and Literature Achievement,' *Research in the Teaching of English* 25.3 (1991): 261–90.

Osberg, Deborah, Gert Biesta, and Paul Cilliers. 'From Representation to Emergence: Complexity's Challenge to the Epistemology of Schooling,' in Mark Mason (ed.), *Complexity Theory and the Philosophy of Education*. Chichester: Wiley-Blackwell, 2008. Pp. 204–17.

Perkins, David. *Smart Schools: Better Thinking and Learning for Every Child*. New York: The Free Press, 1992.

Phelps, Renata. 'The Potential of Reflective Journals in Studying Complexity "In Action",' *Complicity: An International Journal of Complexity and Education* 2.1 (2005): 37–54.

Reif, Frederick. *Applying Cognitive Science to Education: Thinking and Learning in Scientific and Other Domains*. Cambridge, MA: MIT Press, 2008.

Sadler, D. Royce. 'Perils in the Meticulous Specification of Goals and Assessment Criteria,' *Assessment in Education* 14.3 (2007): 387–92.

Semler, L. E. 'The Shakespeare Reloaded Bard Blitz: A Literary Analysis and Essay Building Module,' *mETAphor* 4(2009): 30–44.

Shakespeare, William. *As You Like It.* Arden 3rd edn. Ed. by Juliet Dusinberre. 2006; rpt. London: Thomson, 2007.

——— *Hamlet* (Second Quarto). Arden 3rd edn. Ed. by Ann Thompson and Neil Taylor. London: Thomson, 2006.

——— *King Lear.* Arden 3rd edn. Ed. by R. A. Foakes. 1997; rpt. London: Thomson, 2003.

——— *Shakespeare's Sonnets.* Arden 3rd edn. Ed. by Katherine Duncan-Jones. 1997; rev. London: Methuen, 2010.

——— *The Life and Death of King John.* Ed. by A. R. Braunmuller. 1989; rpt. Oxford: Oxford University Press, 2008.

Sigarev, Vassily. *Ladybird.* Trans. by Sasha Dugdale. London: Royal Court Theatre, 2004.

Smith, Suzanne (reporter). 'HSC Pressures Drive Students to Plagiarise,' *Lateline* TV report. Australian Broadcasting Corporation, broadcast on 11 November 2011.

Stacey, Ralph D. *Complexity and Creativity in Organizations.* San Francisco: Berrett-Koehler, 1996.

——— *Managing the Unknowable: Strategic Boundaries between Order and Chaos in Organizations.* San Francisco: Jossey-Bass, 1992.

——— Douglas Griffin, and Patricia Shaw. *Complexity and Management: Fad or Radical Challenge to Systems Thinking?* 2000; rpt. Abingdon: Routledge, 2006.

Stevenson, Andrew. 'Coaching Culture Needs to End, Say Top HSC Students.' *The Sydney Morning Herald.* 14 December 2011.

Tarricone, Pina. *The Taxonomy of Metacognition.* Hove: Psychology Press, 2011.

Tenner, Edward. *Why Things Bite Back: Technology and the Revenge of Unintended Consequences.* New York: Vintage, 1997.

Tertiary Education Quality and Standards Agency (TEQSA). <http://www.teqsa.gov.au/> Accessed 17 January 2013.

Thompson, Greg, and Ian Cook. 'Manipulating the Data: Teaching and NAPLAN in the Control Society,' *Discourse: Studies in the Cultural Politics of Education* (forthcoming 2014).

Topsfield, Jewel. 'NAPLAN: Is It Worth It?' *Sydney Morning Herald* (26 November 2012).

Torrance, Harry. 'Assessment *as* Learning? How the Use of Explicit Learning Objectives, Assessment Criteria and Feedback in Post-Secondary Education and Training Can Come to Dominate Learning,' *Assessment in Education* 14.3 (2007): 281–94.

Tosey, Paul. 'Interfering with the Interference: An Emergent Perspective on Creativity in Higher Education,' in Norman Jackson, Martin Oliver, Malcolm Shaw, and James Wisdom (eds), *Developing Creativity in Higher Education: An Imaginative Curriculum*. 2006; rpt. Abingdon: Routledge, 2007. Pp. 29–42.

Traub, Valerie. *Desire and Anxiety: Circulations of Sexuality in Shakespearean Drama*. London and New York: Routledge, 1992.

Wenger, Etienne. *Communities of Practice: Learning, Meaning and Identity*. Cambridge: Cambridge University Press, 2008.

INDEX